MW00352992

Protocols:

Handbook
for the female slave

*For Luscious Cat
With Love & Affection
Bob
8/8/08*

Second Edition

Robert J. Rubel, PhD

Protocols:

Handbook
for the female slave

Second Edition

Published by The Nazca Plains Corporation
Las Vegas, Nevada
2007

ISBN: 978-1-887895-12-5

Published by

The Nazca Plains Corporation ®
4640 Paradise Rd, Suite 141
Las Vegas NV 89109-8000

First Edition 2006
Second Edition 2007

Art Director, Blake Stephens
Cover Model, Monique; Text Models, Monique and Elorin
Photography by Corwin
www.photosbyworwin.com

Dedication

Foremost, this book is dedicated to Mistress,
For she has trusted and embraced my Vision,
Thus enabling me even to See this Road.

Next, this book is dedicated to my slave
For she has taken gigantic personal and
Emotional risks to serve me in this Lifestyle.

So, this book is for them, for together
Mistress and my slave have joined me
On my walk down The Road Less Traveled;
And that has made all the difference.

Bob Rubel
2007

The Road Not Taken

Two roads diverged in a yellow wood,
And sorry I could not travel both
And be one traveler, long I stood
And looked down one as far as I could
To where it bent in the undergrowth;

Then took the other, just as fair,
And having perhaps the better claim
Because it was grassy and wanted wear,
Though as for that the passing there
Had worn them really about the same,

And both that morning equally lay
In leaves no step had trodden black.
Oh, I marked the first for another day!
Yet knowing how way leads on to way
I doubted if I should ever come back.

I shall be telling this with a sigh
Somewhere ages and ages hence:
Two roads diverged in a wood, and I,
I took the one less traveled by,
And that has made all the difference.

Robert Frost

Protocols:

Handbook
for the female slave

Robert J. Rubel, PhD

Acknowledgements

I particularly wish to thank three established Leather Masters for allowing me to use their own Protocols as the basis for what has now become this book. My first exposure to Leather Protocols came from Officer Wes, one of my good friends when he lived in Austin and one of my mentors when I went through the Austin Mentors Program. I see him now once or twice a year at Leather conferences, but still feel very close to him. I also thank the Good Officer for his careful and thoughtful reading of the final draft of this book. He made a number of good catches, particularly concerning the concept and application of the Master/slave dynamic.

I have also been heavily influenced by Master Steve Sampson — personally, and also by his Butchmann's Academy website (now APEX – Arizona Power Exchange; see citation on the References page at the end of the book). Here, a wealth of well-organized material formed important parts of my Manual of Protocol and lives on in parts of Chapters 1–4 of this book. Over the ensuing years, I have been drawn to Master Steve, and I make a point of attending his presentations at Leather conferences when I get the chance. We see one another perhaps two times a year.

Finally, a local Leather Master, Master Gary McEntyre, was kind enough to give me a copy of his own Protocol Manual. Many times, I have watched the exquisite public protocols that Master Gary has taught his boy tommy, and it prompted me to ask him if he would share his personal Protocol Manual with me. He did so, and I found many sections in that document that felt exactly right to me. Again, these have been included, here, in their adapted form, principally in chapters 1 and 2.

Thanks to the three of you. You have made a HUGE difference in my life.

In addition to the base material (and impetus) for this book, I again thank two people for writing special sections. First, I thank my slave for preparing the "Courtesan Services" section and for reading the initial and final drafts both for *content edit* and for *line edit,* thus catching numerous places that needed fleshing out. Second, I thank Susan from San Antonio for doing such an outstanding job writing the section on boot and leather care. One look at Charles' boots and I knew I'd found the author for that section.

I also would like to extend a special thanks to koura who did extensive detailed editing to the inital draft of this opus. Thanks to her, readers have a much "smoother" work in their hands.

Bob Rubel
June, 2007

Contents

Preface

If you already own my book entitled *Protocol Handbook for the Leather slave,* be aware that this book is essentially the same book, retitled for different audiences. That said, let's get started with this book.

Every person has at least one passion. It may be origami, sports, medical play or philosophy. Master/slave protocols are my passion. This is my personal manual. At best, it will cover some areas that may help you to create your own protocol manual. If you find value and use in this book, I freely offer it to you.

First and foremost, this is a book written for people who know something about relationships based on Dominance and submission — the BDSM (**B**ondage, **D**iscipline, **S**ado**M**asochism) Lifestyle. If you lack experience in this lifestyle, chances are that you will also lack the context necessary to understand many of its subtleties, as presented in this book. There is really no way around that. But if you DO have experience in power exchange and/or authority exchange, this book is for you.

This book began as a guide for my slave to direct her as she sought to express her love for me through her actions. In this case, her *actions* include her ways of standing, sitting, and speaking (ways of *being),* as well as ways of preparing things to please me, as her "Master" in a consensual "Master/slave" (M/s) relationship.

So, "Why?" you might ask: "Why should I read this book? Why should I be concerned with protocols, neat homes, and elegant meal-service? Why should I care about the lighting in my living room and whether or not there are candles at Table? Why should I care about ways you want YOUR slave to do things?"

The answer, as Larry Townsend so aptly put it in his landmark book *The Leatherman's Handbook* (1972), is that "erotic sensation is never limited to the strictly genital areas; it involves the entire body, utilizing those parts which may have no sexual significance under other circumstances."

So, take the thought that you're setting out on a path of providing *total sensory pleasure,* and marry it to the world of Leather, the world of power exchange (Master/slave relations) and you have an environment in which the Master/Mistress/Dom/Domme has the capacity and power to create a sensual/sexual fantasy world of his/her own making.

(Note: I will discuss the use of Master and Dom later in the book; overall, I will use Master and Dom in a gender-neutral way. That is, rather than clutter the text with Master/Mistress and Dom/Domme I will simply use Master and Dom. No slight is in any way intended towards female Masters or FemDommes. The Protocols described here can be applied whether the Master is male or female and whether the slave is male or female. I'll refer to the slave as "her" or "she" because my slave is female, and this is written for her use.)

To the extent that you want others around you to support the world into which you wish to move, you need to be able clearly to define what you seek. In my experience, if you want *consistently outstanding sexual performance* from your partner, it helps to create a context for the relationship that is "special." My solution to this puzzle has been to create a structure where every day is Valentine's Day. The result has become a sexually blessed life.

So, while on the surface this is a book about *protocols* and *rituals,* it's really about creating the environment, the milieu, that leads to hours of outrageous Leathersex.

Well, that's a good part of it, at any rate. As Guy Baldwin points out, the other half of the equation concerns *transformance.* He notes that the very palpable power underlying Master/slave dynamics is that through the Master/slave (M/s) lifestyle, we enable our slave(s) to let go of their old life and help them build new beliefs. The woman who is now my slave is hardly recognizable in behavior, outlook and appearance to the woman who petitioned to be my slave in the summer of 2003.

I hope you enjoy reading this book as much as I've enjoyed the path it took to get to the place that I could write it.

Introduction

Before We Get Started – Critical Information

This book is intended to be a description of my personal relationship with my own slave. It's written to demonstrate some of the many ways that a modern-day slave can serve his or her Master. This book is intended for those in the M/s lifestyle for whom devotion to the Master is expressed through service.

When entering into a Master/slave relationship, one "hot topic" concerns the slave's training. Most M/s relationships start out with a *collar of consideration*. Other than a temporary *collar of protection,* the collar of consideration is often the first leather collar offered by a Master to a potential slave. After the collar of consideration, many relationships proceed to a *training collar* (indicating a deepening relationship) before a full collar is offered. A full collar signifies a permanent relationship.

In our personal case, we reversed the order of the collars and began with a training collar. As we proceeded in our relationship, training grew deeper and broader. What began as *protocol training* for our public appearances at Leather events grew to include protocols for daily life. Pretty soon the slave learned how to prepare my breakfast, lunch, and dinner in specific ways that I found particularly pleasing. And, as you will soon read, preparing my kind of *dinner* requires significant attention to detail.

So, I began to write it all down so my slave could keep it straight — and now you're holding the result in your hands.

In reality, this is a very detailed manual of *How I Want My Partner to Behave*. Of course, outside of the world of Internal Enslavement, as this practice is sometimes called, this book would be a laughable male pipe dream, the Ultimate Male Fantasy. After all, what woman is going to approach a potential partner and ask: "And how may I change my behavior so that I may please you?" Even if the woman asked such a question, how many men can answer with more than generalities?

So, the content of this book is a little unusual in the world at-large. But in the world of Leather BDSM Master/slave relations, this world of Protocols and Rituals — the contents of this Manual are quite real. This book describes in accurate detail the way I live with my slave.

++++

There is a key point to mention at the beginning of this book: Although both my slave and I are heterosexual, we identify as "Leather." So, let me start by giving my own operating definition of *Leather* and *Not-Leather*. This is *important* because the Protocols that I'll present in this book reflect the Leather perspective. If you have no experience of the Leather Lifestyle, these may be a bit confusing at best, and at worst, strike you as bizarre.

In a general way, the current and diverse "BDSM Community" has developed from two major *paths* in this country. At the risk of oversimplifying these origins for the sake of brevity, the "Leather" path is an outgrowth of returning gay GIs from WWII who paired up with motorcycle gangs in the 1950s and 1960s. They bring *hierarchy, protocol,* and *spirituality* to their modern-day practices. The other BDSM path, a path that I'll refer to as "Not-Leather," evolved out of the Free-Love movement of the 1960s and 1970s. The Leather path has greater focus on obedience and service, where the Not-Leather path has its focus on amorous love.

Of course, these paths cross over at times; there are no absolutes, here. You'll see some of the protocols mentioned in this book practiced among Not-Leather kinksters. You'll find Leatherfolk who don't use many protocols. But in a general sense, there are distinctions. The easiest way to experience the differences between these two BDSM paths is to attend both a "Leather" weekend conference (such as Southplains Leatherfest) and a "Not-Leather" weekend conference (such as Beat Me in St Louis). "How can you spot the differences?" you ask. Well, for starters, are there predominantly gay couples walking around? Are most of the attendees wearing leather vests with "run pins" covering them? If yes, you're at a Leather event.

The Leather BDSM Lifestyle is about Obedience and Service. As wonderwoman wrote in volume I number 1 of the e-zine *Simply Service*, "Obedience is the process of aligning one's behavior with the expectations of another. In a Master/slave relationship, this translates into the process of the slave learning to align her behavior with the expectations of her Master. Obedience is an outward expression of the slave's ability to integrate her trust in and respect for her Master and her belief that he not only knows her well enough to know her best interests, but that he also loves her enough to consistently act on them." That definition is so accurate that I cannot improve upon it.

One of the best articles I've read on the uniqueness of the Leather culture was written by Steve Elliott for a competition that Jack Rinella held back in 2003 (Steve's article took third place). Here, Elliott wrote that those within the Leather culture share four traits in varying degrees: attire, sexuality, community and spirit.

> **Attire** – a strong tendency towards wearing *black.* At Leather gatherings, that might look like black jeans, black "Sam Brown" belt, paratrooper boots, black T-shirt and black vest — with or without "run pins." At more formal Leather events, spit-polished paratrooper boots, black leather pants, etc.

> **Sexuality** – There are a number of books in print about Leathersex. As Elliott points out, it's fundamentally about headspace, power exchange and using the senses. All five of the senses. As Elliott puts it: "...the feel of cold restraints, the smell of sweat, the taste of another's armpit, the sound of a flogger, the look of the leather harness framing a torso." Leathersex involves a more intense level of *connection* than is commonly found in "vanilla" sex ("vanilla" is the term used to denote those who are "not-kinky," who are not within the BDSM community. Thus "vanilla sex" refers to "standard intercourse as practiced by those outside the BDSM Community"). In the Leather world, a person must be in closer touch with oneself and one's partner(s).

> **Community** – Personally, I largely dropped out of the "vanilla" world. I came to socialize almost exclusively with others from

my Community. Elliott points out that this is one of the defining characteristics of Leatherfolk — a tendency to socialize with others who are like us. We go to meetings and play parties with others who share our Leather orientation.

Leather Spirit – Elliott notes that "Leather spirit" transcends attire, sexuality and community. It's the "spiritual core" of this form of BDSM. I don't want to spend a great deal of time on this, but I'll make a brief observation. It is my experience that when Leatherfolk "play," the *toys* (whips, floggers, etc.) are the *vehicles* to take the person *receiving the action* (called the "bottom), as well as the person *administering the action* (called the Top), to a different plane — often with cathartic consequences. In the Not-Leather world, my sense (particularly among those who have been involved only for a few years) is that a flogging is a flogging. A spanking is a spanking: WYSIWYG "what-you-see-is-what-you-get."

By way of summary, one of the often-repeated mythologies is how the heterosexual BDSM community grew out of the Gay Leather culture. That mythology is not exactly accurate. Robert Bienvenu in his doctoral dissertation on the origins of BDSM both in Europe and in the US (www. americanfetish.net) reports that there were historically two cultures in the U.S. — gay and heterosexual. The swinging community gave the heterosexual SM culture (which was well in place long before the 60s) additional means of contacting one another. However, neither the gay nor the het culture knew about the other, and each developed in different ways. Thus, many Leathermen thought (and still think) they were the origin of it all. (Thanks to Master Bert Cutler for bringing Dr. Bienvenu's work to my attention.)

Because of these different beginnings, the "feel" of these two BDSM cultures is quite different — though both cultures are now somewhat pansexual. In the broadest sense, the Leather BDSM culture has a structure, formality and spirituality that is largely absent from the Not-Leather BDSM culture.

+++

My final opening note is to say that to give you a robust feel for this Lifestyle, I have endeavored to combine fact, philosophy, pragmatism and commentary. In most cases, after I provide the protocol, I will comment on why that protocol is the way it is in an attempt to help those who want a better understanding of this M/s subculture.

This work began as my personal *Manual of Protocol* for my slave. One day when I was working on this project, a senior Leatherman happened to be at my home. He asked what I was writing and we started discussing it. He noted that Masters frequently don't know exactly HOW they want to be served and that he knew of no current book that addressed this issue. Furthermore, he thought this broad treatment would be a valuable addition to the Leather literature. (He also commented that most slaves would probably appreciate some guidance about the more formal service covered in this book, better to please their Masters.) After more discussion, he suggested that I convert my Manual of Protocol into a book format and publish it. Ultimately, I agreed to do that.

What This Book Is

This book is my personal *Manual of Protocol* for my slave. This book guides her behavior, whether or not she is in my presence.

Often, those fairly new to BDSM have a vague sense that M/s relationships are somehow better than D/s relationships and in a universe different from Top/bottom play. That is not so, it's just that they are *different.*

As Master Skip Chasey points out, Top/bottom play is about the physical body, Dominant/submissive play is about the mental body and Master/slave relationships are about the spiritual body. Master Steve Sampson cuts it slightly differently: "Top and bottom play is about the *sexual self*; dominance and submission is about *energy* and Master/slave relationships are about the *spiritual.*"

As **obedience** and **service** are at the core of the Master/slave dynamic, *protocols* become the means by which the slave aligns himself or herself with Master's choices for personal service. In that light, each Master has to create protocols that enable his or her slave to express obedience through tailored service. "Slave training" is all about teaching the slave to perform that service.

Now, there is a great deal of fantasy built up about Master/slave relations, particularly about slave training. Often, these fantasies have something to do with, "Do what I say, or I'll punish you." That line of thought is foreign to me. My slave is a person. A vibrant and intelligent person. My slave probably has a higher IQ than I do and has substantial advanced training in skill areas that support our relationship. With her slaveheart, my slave's primary purpose is to serve me. My role, as Master, is to train her in ways of providing that service. It's a long process, the result of which is that those who knew her before she entered the Lifestyle and still know her today find her vastly changed.

I have never punished her for a lapse in Protocol. When a glitch occurs, I point it out, and we discuss it. My method of training — true, long-term modification of her behavior — rests on reinforcing positive behaviors and downplaying the glitches. I approach *training* in this way because if I were to keep picking on the glitches, she would become hypercritical of her own actions and become anxious when around me.

So, why are these my opening paragraphs? Because this is a book written from my heart about a real, live, ongoing, dynamic Master/slave relationship. This is not a fantasy. M/s fantasies are very different from actuality. This takes daily work. This takes daily practice. This takes commitment to the road less traveled.

Far more than a book of Protocols, this book presents a look into the BDSM Leather subculture as a whole. I have provided a *Commentary* after most of the protocols in order to relate them to the larger Purpose of the described activity. That is, the *Commentary* explains the "why" of the Protocol.

Absent the commentaries, this book instructs my slave how to behave in public, and in private, how to serve me. Everything in this book is actively used in my relationship with my slave.

This gives me a good way to transition to the next idea: There are many, many ways to approach Master/slave (M/s) relationships. Ultimately, a couple must develop protocols and rituals that support *who they are*. This book describes my protocols for my slave, and is not intended to be the final word for any other M/s relationship.

Because I am somewhat intense and "driven" in my life, these protocols reflect that personality. The level of detail I specify for my slave would be incomprehensible to many other M/s couples; it would get in the way of their relationship. On the other hand, some other couples may prefer even more rigor and detail in their lives together than I've expressed in this book. I am not offering a blueprint, but a snapshot of an ongoing and vital M/s relationship.

By way of summary, then, this book describes who my slave and I are together. And our behaviors *together* are an outgrowth of who we are in the world.

As I took my slave further into training, I wanted her to learn butlering skills. But I could only find one or two books on the subject; I couldn't find specific written material designed to instruct a person in how to *serve*. I was able to find a few unpublished examples of protocol manuals written by Leathermen for their boys, and while these were extremely helpful in relation to speaking, standing and sitting protocols, none of these went into the wide range of *service* I had in mind for my slave.

So, I started reading etiquette books and thinking about how I wanted my slave to act.

Ultimately, I decided on a path of training that recreates her as my *Personal Assistant* (the female form of a butler combined with service as an executive secretary and valet). These protocols, then, are part of ongoing training materials designed to shape my slave into my *Personal Assistant* — with benefits.

What This Book is NOT

First, this book is not our **Contract**. Our Contract defines the terms and conditions of our *Relationship*. This book defines the slave's *behavior*.

Second, this book of personal protocols is not generalizable. That is, you — the reader — are not likely to want the same out of your slave that I want from my slave. However, this material should give you ideas to help you design your own Protocol Manual. For example, your idea of a great weekend activity may be to curl up on your living room couch and watch a ball game. In that case, you may wish to design a series of protocols that govern how your popcorn is served to you, the temperature of your beer, and how each is served to you.

This book does NOT purport to represent any other Masters' protocols or rituals for their slaves. There are as many ways of approaching an M/s relationship as there are people practicing these activities. Guy Baldwin, in *Ties that Bind*, observes: "I have seen a Master with several slaves. Some slaves have more than one Master. Some slaves have slaves, and some Masters are themselves slaves to yet other Masters. Another slave I know has a lover (mostly vanilla) and a Master as well…" Personally, I know of an instance where the slave's Owner and the slave's Master are different people; the slave has been allowed a Master for a particular purpose.

What I have captured in this Manual/book are simply beliefs, activities, and behaviors that fit *who we are* as people and as a couple. There are many Paths within this Lifestyle. You, as a Master or a slave, must select your own. I will also add that this is not a manual that explains how we behave with our biological families. We match the standards of the family member present, especially in regards to minors.

And this is a Leather book — it may or may not *resonate* with you. The tone and temper of this book reflects the highly structured Leather culture in which I feel at home. A Not-Leather BDSM Master/slave relationship is likely to be quite different. And, of course, there are other models, such as the Gorean M/s model, about which I know nothing beyond whispers and innuendos.

Definitions: Etiquette, Protocol and Ritual

Etiquette represents a set of rules that guide us toward the polite way of interacting with others in the world. Etiquette is culture-bound and situation-bound. For example, you can imagine that "proper etiquette" among inmates in a U.S. Federal prison is a world apart from "proper etiquette" among students of a private British boarding school. At its core, *etiquette* represents a way of showing respect toward others while demonstrating your understanding of good manners.

Protocols represent a set of rules that govern specific actions or behavior in a particular situation. So, there is a "lockdown protocol" in prison and a "test-taking protocol" in the boarding school.

In terms of our BDSM lifestyle, "etiquette" can be said to be *outward looking* — it's describing the way you interact with others within our culture. "Protocols," however, are *inward looking;* they describe the way the Master wishes his/her slave to do specific things within the M/s structure. Protocols enhance our play and relationships with structure, ritual and symbols.

Rituals are like traditions — ways that we choose to do things that are repeated with some regularity, but without a set of rules that govern specific behavior. For example, when it's cool enough outside to have a fire in the fireplace, my evening ritual is to have appetizers and a drink with my slave in front of the fireplace while my computer-driven piano (whom I refer to as *Harvey* — remember the invisible rabbit in the movie with Jimmy Stewart?) plays for us. It's not a protocol; it's a ritual.

How Protocols Come to Be
Protocols are an outgrowth of a Master's values.

A Master who most values honesty and integrity may create protocols focused on these. A Master who values sitting in front of a television drinking beer and eating popcorn, may develop protocols about the temperature of the beer, how it's served to him and how the popcorn comes to be placed beside him.

The things that I personally value will become crystal clear as you read this book. But that doesn't mean that YOU will value them or be interested in the protocols I've built around them. The best I can offer is a solid example of an internally congruous Manual of Protocol that I actually use with my slave.

Masters, after all, are Eagles. They build their own worlds; they don't flock to emulate worlds created by others.

Why Use Protocols?

So, "Why use protocols?"

First, protocols turn routine actions into "defined, repeatable events," to use business-speak. It's like going to a chain restaurant. Whether you're in Los Angeles or Boston, the food preparation and presentation will be virtually identical. Similarly, if I ask my slave to do something for me, I can be assured that she will do that action exactly according to our protocols, regardless of the circumstances surrounding my request. I can relax and not concern myself about how my slave will act/react. Because I've written out and taught my slave how to behave in most common situations, I need no longer concern myself with micromanaging her. This frees me and enables me to relax around her in ways that have seldom been possible in non-M/s relationships.

Second, protocols focus the mind and declare our mutual *intention* to be fully present — body, mind and spirit — for what is about to take place, and to clearly declare that intention through stylized action.

Third, protocols make a relationship **special**. "Protocols in action" communicate to the other person — and to anyone watching — just how valued this relationship is. One of the reasons this book presents such *formal* protocols is because it stresses this point: in my world, dinner is not just a time to eat food, it's a time to celebrate the uniqueness of my relationship with my slave.

I am reminded of the 2004 motion picture *50 First Dates* with Adam Sandler and Drew Barrymore. The female character (Lucy Whitmore) had been in a car accident with the result that her memory self-erased every 24 hours. The male character, Henry Roth, set out on a mission to make Lucy fall in love with him anew every single day — for every single day was a new meeting for Lucy. In my M/s relationship with my slave, I fall in love with her every single night we are together when she comes to me Dressed and in High Protocol. It's magic. It's like nothing else I've ever experienced — and happens night after night.

How this Book is Constructed

About the Writing Style

A brief word about writing style: I'm an educational sociologist by training. Within my specialty, I've published two academic books and over 30 articles for professional journals. Traditionally, these tomes are written in third-person, passive voice and tend to put people to sleep. I'm not going to subject non-academic readers to this style. So, I'm writing this in first-person active voice; when I write a "commentary," I'm speaking directly to you.

I've interspersed *commentaries* throughout this book at the end of most of the sections. It explains the "why" of that section or "why I want that particular protocol."

Oh — and I LOVE A.A. Milne's *Winnie the Pooh* books and will sometimes Capitalize Odd Words by way of applying Emphasis. It's harmless. Having started my career as a high school English teacher, I know that I can get away with it.

Objectification

On a more controversial point, I recognize that SlaveMaster (and other highly regarded Leather Masters) refer to their slaves as "it" (an object) better to bring *ego surrender* to the fore. I have considered this and am not ready at this time to embrace this concept and action. I continue to refer to my slave as "her" or "she" because her personality, her *being,* is an essential part of what she gives to me. But I am keeping an open mind on this topic.

About Chapter One

Chapter One sets the *context for slavery* for my slave. This is critical material, for without it, she may not share common understandings with me about the M/s dynamic. Not all readers will agree with what I have written and that is somewhat beside the point. It just makes sense for each Master to consider the context in which the relationship should develop, refining and discussing this with his/her slave before advancing too far into the *relationship* that precedes the definition and use of *protocols.*

Commentary: This is one of the paragraphs containing a "sleeper." Let me draw attention to the last line, above; **relationship precedes protocols**.

In my experience, a Dom will sometimes start M/s negotiations with a woman **before he has spent time with her to establish their mutual desire to form a basic relationship.** When the Dom starts right in with M/s negotiations without knowing the candidate very well, these negotiations often crater — or the relationship begins, but the slave gets released early from the training contract.

A defining difference between "Leather" and "Not-Leather" is that in the **Leather world**, the slave usually petitions the Master, not the other way around. Through his demonstrable mastery and public service, the Master attracts slave candidates. Typically, the Leather Master will ask the slave candidate what the slave brings to the table — what the slave candidate knows or can do that will benefit the Master. These are threshold questions. The couple must establish that they WANT an M/s relationship — and to do that, they must spend time getting to know one another. If there's a fit, the couple can then begin more detailed negotiations about entering into a training contract. (See sample in Appendix A)

Chapter 1

Common Understandings in Common Settings

Core Concepts of M/s Relations

In an M/s relationship, the Master consensually owns the slave in the same way he owns a cherished pet. With the acceptance of her permanent collar, the slave and Master enter an exchange of *total obedience and service* on the slave's part and responsibility for *emotional, physical, social, spiritual and financial well-being* on the Owner/Master's part.

This section expresses *how* you, the slave, will learn the level of obedience and service that I require.

As with all areas of mastery, the SLAVE'S mastery of her role within a Master/slave relationship is based upon:

- Consistency
- Focus
- Mindset

Through *consistent use,* the protocols in this book are intended — through *focus* — *to* produce the *mindset* I seek in my slave.

The Nature of our Relationship

The principal activity of this slave is the exchange of services in return for structure, security and direction. For the sake of *public appearances* outside of the Leather Community, my slave will be referred to as my "Personal Assistant." (*Personal Assistant* is the term used to describe a female butler who also serves as an executive secretary and valet.)

The slave's overriding requirements are:

> **To obey my Instructions;**
> **To anticipate and solve My problems;**
> **To serve with grace and elegance.**

Generally, the slave is to gain such skills as to be able to bring me:

- Formal personal service at table and throughout the day;
- Sexual pleasure orally, vaginally, anally and manually;
- Evening entertainment pleasure through music or reading aloud;
- Social entertainment through dancing;
- Visual pleasure through the slave's physical appearance both clothed and naked; and
- Sensual pleasure through use of perfumes and scents.

Commentary: So, what's going on, here? And what does the slave get out of it? I've already alluded to Master's responsibilities, covered later in more detail. Right now, I've simply let the slave know what I expect out of OUR deal together. This is a "make it or break-it" moment. This is what I am seeking in a slave — my "position statement."

Distinction between Master and Dom

In the Leather world, "Master" is an achieved rank. Generally, a Master is recognized in a public ceremony for service within the community. Henceforth, other recognized Masters refer to this person as a Master. In this manual the term Master describes the Leather relationship between Bob and his slave. **However, the use of the term "Master" in this work is not intended to suggest that I am an acknowledged Leather Master**.

Dom is a role designation more commonly used in the "Not-Leather" world. "Dom" describes a psychological role of one person in relation to another. While few Doms are Leather Masters, all Leather Masters are dominant males or dominant females.

Distinction between D/s and M/s

As Master Skip Chasey and Master Steve Sampson point out, D/s (Dominance and submission) is anchored in the mental body; D/s involves *power exchange* and is usually time-delimited. M/s is anchored in the spiritual body; M/s involves *authority exchange* and is a way of being. Power exchange is used during a scene or during the time when the D/s couple is together; M/s is a lifestyle choice and behaviors continue even when the Master and slave are not together. I will explain the power dynamics of these relationships in more detail below.

> **Commentary:** This book will be read by people who identify as "Leather," as well as people who do not identify as "Leather." Although many who do not identify as Leather refer to themselves using the terms Master and slave, because they do not come from a tradition where the title of Master is earned, I prefer to use the words "Dom" and "sub" when referring to them. This is not intended to put them down but simply to distinguish between the two approaches to BDSM. For that reason, some sentences will say: "...when the Master or Dom..." This is not a mistake: I identify as Leather. I want my slave to identify as Leather and understand the distinction, and it is my impression that in the traditional world of Leather, the term "Dom" is not often used to refer to a Leatherman.

The Nature of a slave

As I mentioned in the preface, many ideas in this book came originally from material available from the APEX Academy/Butchmann's website and are used here with permission. The next paragraphs are classic examples that I cannot improve upon.

"A slave is a man or woman who has a special heart — a heart that requires a connection with another person in order to find completeness in their life. A person is born with slave heart — he cannot be "made" into a slave nor can wishing to be one bring it about. It is a natural state. A slave may actualize their destiny by choosing to live in obedience to another person's will and to serve that person — their Master or Mistress — in obedience. Most slaves are very bright and capable, and they may make many decisions every day affecting other people, large sums of money, important projects, and so on. But slaves generally do not make decisions easily or well that concern themselves, and that is one of the reasons they seek a Master — to form that point of centered-ness from which to live their lives.

"Someone may have "heart of slave" and be on a journey toward actualizing their destiny without yet having found the Master their heart tells them to give their life to. And others may feel drawn toward slavery but not yet know their hearts. For simplicity, all of the above will be referred to as "slave" in this protocol.

"Once a slave truly understands that their existence is more complete and fulfilled in being obedient, everything else falls into place. A slave speaks in order to convey requested information or to request information about the Master's intentions. A slave eats, sleeps, washes, exercises, takes medication, and so on in order to remain healthy and available for service. slaves labor at tasks assigned by their Master or hold an outside job so that they can contribute to the Master's household and not be a financial burden. Anything a slave is allowed to do for personal gratification is a gift from their Master, not a right. When this aspect of slave heart is realized, slaves start to find peace in their lives." (Butchmann's material: What is a slave?)

> **Commentary:** My message, here, is that if you indeed have a slave heart, you will not feel comfortable in a relationship that does not respect that **authority exchange**.

Distinction Between "Power Exchange" and "Authority Exchange"

When the Dom accepts power from the submissive and the submissive gives up power to the Dom, this is referred to as a **power exchange**. When the submissive is away from the Dominant, she is free to resume control of her world. This is not so with **authority exchange**.

Authority exchange is the basis of an M/s (Master/slave) relationship. The slave permanently (or at least during the contract period) gives up authority over him/herself to the Master. "What kind of authority?" you ask. The authority to make willful decisions. For example, depending upon the structure of the relationship, it can mean that the slave no longer controls decisions about how to use **time** or **money**. Authority does NOT change hands when the slave is out of contact with her Master. It's a core concept of the M/s dynamic and one of the reasons it is so crucial to delineate the boundaries of the relationship during contract negotiations. **You get what you negotiate.** If the slave needs to maintain authority over a particular area of her life, this must be spelled out before either the Master or slave can honestly enter the agreement. Provisions should always be made in the contract for renegotiations when unforeseen situations arise and to allow for growth of the relationship.

Who is This slave?
The slave is a person whose personal identity and sense of self is fulfilled through service and obedience to another person. To resonate in this relationship, the slave consents to give up extensive personal freedoms in exchange for extraordinary protection.

This slave does not have rights other than those granted by her Master. The slave does not have the right to be upset by an order or Instruction. The slave does not have the right to prepare coffee or foods for herself without asking permission. The slave's whole reason for being is to make Master's life more pleasant, ordered and efficient. **To the extent that the slave's purpose in doing anything is for herself and not for her Master, that poses a direct conflict with the slave's reason for being.**

The slave has no right to make time demands of Master. The slave is used whenever Master needs the particular services that slave has to offer. The slave has no personal Time unless her Master grants it.

This slave is NOT Master's "girlfriend." A "girlfriend" is a person with the same rights and responsibilities as her partner; the slave is property and has only those rights given her by her Master. A "girlfriend" might say: "Hey, I want to go see this movie. Let's go out to dinner and catch the show." The slave will say: "Master, if it Pleases you, there is a movie I think you would enjoy. May I have permission to describe it to you?"

Commentary: There is quite an active controversy within the M/s movement about the role of "love." On the one hand, some Masters take the position that "love" contaminates the M/s dynamic because Master can never be sure whether the slave is complying with a request/Instruction out of <u>love</u> or out of <u>obedience</u>. Since obedience is the core of the M/s dynamic, Master would lose the capacity to monitor the slave's core reactions.

On the flip side, many Masters feel that if they're going to put all the time and effort into training a slave with whom they will spend lots of time, they want to be submerged in a loving relationship with that person. But a loving relationship is not necessarily a girlfriend/boyfriend relationship, and the Master may want to carefully consider whether to suppress the tendency for slaves to think of their Master as their "girlfriend" or "boyfriend." "Girlfriend/boyfriend" relationships belong to the Vanilla World along with other family members (especially children), and do not involve the authority or power exchanges inherent in D/s and M/s relationships.

There can be substantial differences between "the Master's love" and "the slave's love." The Master is more likely to love the slave than be "in love" with the slave. However, the slave will probably fall "in love" with Master. It may be useful to discuss different forms of love with a prospective slave, lest they confuse your relationship.

How is This slave to Think of herself?

"A slave's reference to [herself] is understood to mean the part of [her] Master, or [her] Master's property, that consists of the slave's body, mind, and spirit. When a slave says (or writes) 'i,' it refers to the body and energies of the slave, but not [her] will, which as long as she is in service is obedient to that of [her] Master. When a slave says 'my' or 'mine,' it means that part of the Master's property that is in the slave's keeping or stewardship — except, of course, in the phrases 'my Master or Mistress,' 'my slave brother or sister,' or 'my slavery' (the only thing that truly belongs to a slave). (Butchmann's: Forms of Address.)

How Does this slave Fit into our Family Structure?

If another woman is present who is not of the Leather culture, the slave will serve Master and will not serve this other woman. This other woman will serve herself or be served by Master, as proper decorum dictates.

If another Leatherslave is present and participating with us in a Leather scene involving an evening meal, then the slave will take on First Girl responsibilities and the visiting Leatherslave will serve Master through my slave. Later, in the "Dining Protocols" section of this book, I explain the "Order of Precedence" charts that govern serving order.

Rules Governing Family Relations

This Family can be viewed as a "team" in the business sense of the word. Many of the *rules and guidelines* for building strong teams apply equally for building a strong Family. In summary, they are:

- **Be loyal to those not present**. Family members will not discuss Family issues with Others. No personal information about Family members will be shared with Others. Parenthetically, if the slave hears someone speaking ill of another, my preference is that the slave suggest that they find a way to discuss it directly and constructively with the person.

- **Don't complain to Others.** If the slave has a concern or complaint, she will bring it to me. Concerns and complaints will receive a better reception if they are presented as facts/issues devoid of emotion and spin. That is, there is an "issue" and there is the "story about the issue." I'm not interested in the story.

- **Do more than your fair share.** I recognize that much is required of my slave. But that's the nature of the deal. While I'm working very hard to create a Magical World filled with intellectual and emotional stimulation, I need my slave to be searching relentlessly for ways of helping.

- **Be dependable.** Be where I expect her to be, when I expect her to be there, prepared to do the job-at-hand.

- **Anticipate what I am going to do next.** Good Family members rarely need to tell one another what to do next because the partner is already doing it.

- **Be flexible.** Mistress and I tend to act quickly once we understand a situation. My slave must be prepared to follow quickly, and without slowing us down. My slave must learn to recognize when Mistress and I are in "problem-solving" mode and learn to interject refining questions at that time — not *after* we've made a decision.

The slave's Obligations

In rank order, the slave's obligations are to his or her
- Biological family
- Master
- Leather Family
- Local Leather Community
- Leather Tribe

Master's Responsibilities

Master is responsible for the slave's mental, physical, social, financial, and spiritual well-being. Master is responsible always to do what is for the highest good of the slave. A Master is responsible for the slave's welfare, I therefore instruct her to meet her obligations to her biological family.

In the larger sense, Master will behave as what Master Skip Chasey calls a "Servant Master" with respect to his slaves, in essence serving them in many ways, so that they are best able to follow their inner Natures as they develop and mature.

Commentary: Being the Master in an M/s relationship involves a lot of hard work. Much of the Master's role is to support the slave's own personal growth at the same time that he trains the slave to serve him perfectly. In my Family, we actively participate in Leather and BDSM seminars, workshops, and groups both as participants and as presenters. We have also attended a number of the Landmark Education Forum series of courses, designed for personal growth and life coaching. We do this better to understand ourselves and better to understand and communicate with one another, in addition to honing and developing our skills and abilities.

Concepts Specifically Relating to My slave

In this relationship, Protocols represent an important means to demonstrate service and obedience on a daily basis. Protocols are a way for the slave to "come present" with her slavery. Mastering the Protocols is something like mastering a dance form; it takes daily practice and focused concentration until the movements and processes become second nature.

Grace, Elegance and Lucidity

Master seeks to build an environment that exudes grace and elegance.

- The slave is responsible for identifying and employing ways of incorporating graceful movement into her presentation and style.

- The slave is expected to have and to use high-level language skills. She will use correct grammar and develop a vocabulary commensurate at least with that of a person entering graduate school.

- The slave is responsible for learning a pleasing vocal tonality, modulating her voice, and enunciating her words.

- The slave is responsible for being sensitive to her dress and appearance at all times. In our Family, the slave is expected to be *slightly overdressed* on all public occasions.

Commentary: The concepts expressed in this section represent one of my "Core Values." I'm not interested in having sloppy service or sloppy people around me. When I go out in public, I'm neatly dressed; I expect my slave to be as well or better dressed than I am. As a former English teacher, I'm not interested in hearing "butchered English" from my slave.

The Concept of Sprezzatura

"Sprezzatura" is an Italian word meaning effortless technique. The slave will view this concept as the byword, the key concept, underlying all actions. In this Household, everything is to look effortless; meals are to come together on time and perfectly.

> **Commentary:** True mastery is often evinced by the apparent ease with which the practitioner carries out a function or task. In my Household, I expect the slave to be so competent at tasks that others observing will not see or be distracted by the **work** or **effort** involved.

Service

In the broadest sense, the slave is always to be serving the *idea* or *concept* of the Relationship, seen through proxies such as:

- Physical appearance and bearing;
- Following specified exercise routines;
- Orderliness of the home and the car.

> **Commentary:** There are certain behaviors that carry beyond times when the slave is physically with Master. In our case, I care how my slave looks and how neat her car appears. I'm not comfortable around clutter, and I grew up in a culture where the women were always coiffed and dressed — particularly to go shopping or to get on an airplane. Also, I care that my slave does not appear hurried when in public. I require a graceful gait. My slave knows how to take her seat like a lady.

Master's Expectations of the slave

Correctness in Public and Private

"A slave will always act and respond in such a way as to make the Master's orders look 'right.' A slave will never give the appearance that he thinks a Master has made a mistake, whether by facial expression, body language, or verbal challenge. Masters are not perfect, but whatever They order is 'right' because it is their will. It is the Master's will that the slave submits to, not his correctness. If the slave feels that she has information the Master is lacking, or sees a better possibility that He has not considered, the slave may — within the limits of the protocol — ask whether Master wishes her to convey such information or to make a suggestion." (Butchmann's, Obedience and Correctness)

In like manner, Master will refrain from publicly pointing out or making an issue of a slave's service gaffes. It is embarrassing to both the slave and to bystanders, and it can interfere with the slave's *slaveheart,* resulting in further deterioration of service. Any correction will be done in private, away from others' eyes and ears. The slave is consensually owned and her feelings must be taken into account.

If the situation involves potential or imminent peril to the life, health or safety of any individual, then the slave must act immediately and without regard to protocol.

Additionally, Master may not force the slave to commit any unlawful or patently unsafe act.

> **Commentary:** While I believe this section is quite clear, I know of an instance that occurred recently within my local community where negotiations about establishing an M/s relationship broke down over this point. After an insensitive "correction in public" a breach of trust surfaced that even third party assistance failed to mend, despite the fact that the breach was extremely minor. The offending party couldn't/wouldn't recognize the breach as a serious trust issue within the context of the emerging relationship.

Reliability Builds Trust

The business world speaks of "defined repeatable processes." In my M/s relationship, I expect the slave to perform her tasks the same way each time. After all, what else is a Protocol?

For the slave, following requests, directives or Instructions combines many positive attributes, including faithful obedience, respect, dedication and trust. My orders are not questioned; clarification may be requested if appropriate.

I expect my slave to exhibit the attributes of honesty, punctuality and dedication.

- **Honesty.** Being honest at all times will maximize our understanding of one another. The slave will avoid passive-aggressive behaviors, as these combine two unattractive traits: dishonesty and unwillingness to communicate directly.

- **Dedication.** By nature, this is destined to be an intense relationship. It takes dedication and commitment to keep it going.

- **Punctuality.** Naturally this applies to any commitment, but particularly to promptly returning phone calls and email.

  o If we are meeting in town, the slave will take care to arrive early; she is not to keep Master waiting and will be corrected for so doing.

  o If the slave suspects that she will be unable to keep a time commitment, the slave must reach Master by phone to explain the delay and recommit to a revised arrival time.

Commentary: "Being on time" is one of my core values. It is an expression of respect, an expression of one's personal integrity — one's ability to keep one's word. One of the very few areas that will make me angry involves "being late" without notifying me ahead of time and revising her expected arrival time.

Continuing Education

My slave is expected to continue to grow emotionally and academically. From time to time, Master will enroll her in outside coursework meant to broaden her outlook on life and/or her skills.

Commentary: Knowing that I would require more from my slave than her existing level of competence, I took great care not to alarm her early in our relationship. I slowly revealed the depth and breadth of training that would be required. After three years she has come to understand that I will enroll her in outside (commercial) training courses, seminars and classes for many, many years to come. As examples, our Family takes various self-help/communication courses, dance classes, music lessons, and so forth. We are a "cerebral" Family that likes to grow into new areas of interest.

Openness

"slaves exist without privacy or defenses. What they are, whatever they do, and even what they think and feel must be open for inspection at all times. slaves should always carry themselves with dignity, whether naked and in chains or out in the workaday world, and their appearance and behavior should always reflect positively on their Master and their slave brothers and sisters." (Butchmann's: Openness)

Availability – Cell Phone Contact

The slave is to be available 100% of the time, 24/7 by cell phone except during such times the slave has petitioned a proposed "period of unavailability" for Master to consider. There is simply no "normal time during the day or night" that the slave is to be unreachable. This includes times when Master and slave are out together, for instance, in different parts of the same store. Master must be able to contact the slave whenever he so desires.

Failure to keep the cell phone on the slave's person at all times will result in a Consequence.

> **Commentary:** This point is important in my life. I am busy and focused. If I need to reach my slave, I need to reach her NOW. I do not want to have to add a "re-contact slave" note to my list of tasks for the day. This is one of the few areas wherein I permit no latitude. To avoid becoming stressed over this point, I have instructed my slave to notify me of any times during the day that she cannot be reached. Typically, this includes her exercise period and before she begins any meetings at her workplace.

Safewords

When in Play, Master will employ RACK (rather than SSC) standards.

When NOT in play, the slave will use Master's given name as an emotional safeword. That is, if the slave is in a conversation with Master and encounters an emotional landmine, using Master's given name will be interpreted by Master as a conversation-stopping event. It is interpreted as calling "RED."

When the slave is permitted to play with other Masters, Doms or Tops, she is *required* to play under SSC rules unless express permission has been granted by Master to play under RACK rules. The slave should not expect that such permission would ever be granted.

> **Commentary:** This is not a trivial point. I agree with those within the Community who feel that the "Safe, Sane and Consensual" rules give scene-control to the bottom. After all, use of safewords in the SSC setting suggest that the bottom knows better than Master what's good for him/herself. There are a number of "problems" with this setup. First, when a bottom goes into sub-space, it is unlikely that he or she can even call "red." So the whole structure is defeated. Second, in Leathersex, much of the play is intended to produce catharsis. The bottom is unlikely to be able to move to that state if he/she has to monitor whether or not the play is getting too intense to be processed. Again, the SSC structure fails.
>
> For these reasons, we play by RACK standards: RACK stands for Risk-Aware Consensual Kink. Within the Community, it's assumed that you're very experienced before you will play with someone under RACK rules. Playing by RACK standards assumes that the Master knows the slave (or other bottom) so well that Master can read body language and other non-verbal cues and will take the necessary actions to avoid causing harm. There are no safewords in the RACK schema.

Requests, Orders and Instructions

The slave will attend particularly to the word "Instruction." An "Instruction" is a special term in our Relationship. An Instruction is a Command that brooks no interference. If I am so focused on the slave doing something that I issue an Instruction, be assured that the slave is Wide Awake and taking notes. An Instruction usually carries with it a requirement to report progress to me. Consequences for failure always accompany an Instruction. This is not at all true for a "request" and seldom true for an "order." (Note: a "consequence" involves a "correction," not a "punishment." As I'll discuss later, *punishments* are only invoked for contract violations, not for protocol violations.)

Here are some examples of each form.

- **Request:** "Please bring me some coffee."

- **Order:** "I'd like you to be Dressed and ready to entertain our Guests at 7pm tomorrow night."

- **Instruction:** "This is an Instruction: you are to keep the interior of your car completely free from clutter and keep the outside of your car washed. At no time will I enter your car if there is clutter in the passenger compartments."

Commentary: I've had a love-affair with words my entire life. I am particularly attentive to the connotation of certain words. For example, one **talks to** a class or group of people and **speaks with** an individual. In my world, "talking" is rather one-sided; "speaking" is two-sided. This section sets forth distinctions that are vital in my M/s Relationship with my slave. For example, much of what I do with my slave when she is in service involves "talking to," in the sense that I am not inviting comment or conversation from her. On the other hand, when she is fulfilling "Courtesan" activities, we are very much speaking with one another.

Required to Comply

Regardless of the closeness of the relations between Master and the slave, this slave is admonished to remember always that she is still a slave and subject to Master's will. In that light, the slave is required to comply with our *Contract* and with my orders and Instructions.

In my world, there is a distinction between *correction* and *punishment.*

- Correction is the opportunity to understand more fully the importance Master places on a Protocol or behavior. Typically, correction is administered when the slave is learning a task or a procedure and — despite a few reminders — doesn't get it right.

- Punishment is administered for failure to comply either with the Contract or with the policies and procedures in this document when that failure is due to willfulness or negligence on the slave's part. Punishment is the opportunity to atone for failure. The incident that gave rise to the punishment will then be *forgiven* and not be spoken of again following the punishment debriefing. The slate is wiped clean.

Commentary #1: For example, if the slave is a passenger in my car and forgets to wait for me to come around and open the door for her, the slave should expect to be swatted on the ass. Of course, when she wants to be swatted, she simply opens the car door, but that's another story. At any rate, I endeavor to make "corrections" light-hearted and fun. The intention is to get the slave's attention and focus.

Commentary #2: No action or inaction by my slave has ever arisen requiring Punishment. In our three years together, I've invoked the "consequences clause" 4–6 times. Generally, a word about the problem or concern is sufficient. There are two reasons I don't often correct my slave. First, she is very focused on being a perfect slave; and second, if she starts getting the idea that she can't do anything **right**, anxiety will creep into the relationship. An anxious slave will make more mistakes, leading to more correction, leading to more anxiety. When this happens in a relationship, it often leads to a break up.

In our relationship, I'm interested in catching my slave "doing right," not doing wrong. Following from that, most of my "corrections" are light-hearted. By contrast, Punishments aren't fun and certainly aren't funny.

Willful or Negligent Failure to Comply

The rare instances where the slave acts in a willful or negligent manner will result in punishment.

- No punishment will be undertaken when Master is angry.

- Before administering punishment, the slave will have the opportunity to fully explain how this Failure occurred.

- Master will ask the slave to recommend her Punishment.

- Master will listen to the slave's proposal and, after consideration, determine the correct course of punishment. Master will inform the slave of his decision.

- Master will use the minimum influence necessary to compel the slave's compliance with the policies and procedures the slave previously agreed to.

- Bearing in mind that Master wishes the Relationship to continue, there are no limits to the nature or extent of punishment that could be ordered as a result of the slave's act of willfulness or negligence so long as no crime is committed (battery, death). In reality, in our relationship, *punishment* takes the path of restrictive Instructions about the use of slave's time and/or withdrawal of the slave's Time with Master.

- After punishment has been administered, Master and slave will sit down and discuss changes that may be needed in the relationship to ensure that such a breach does not occur again.

Commentary #1: An underlying assumption of the M/s dynamic is that the slave is in Internal Enslavement and will do everything possible to serve and obey to the best of his or her ability. Thus, a **willful** or **negligent** action must be taken for what it is: a cry for help by the slave. That is, the slave must be trying to get your attention through bad behavior, having failed to get your attention any other way.

Commentary #2: In the world of BDSM M/s theory, it is generally agreed that one doesn't punish with toys used for play. That is, if you normally spank or flog or whip the slave for play, it's not appropriate to use those same instruments for punishment. On the other hand, you can purchase special floggers or whips or canes that are ONLY USED for punishment.

Commentary #3: Personally, I believe that psychological punishment is more effective than physical punishment and this Protocol reflects my belief.

Reality Checks

With my business background, I firmly believe in "action-evaluation feedback loops." In the same way that I used to have *performance reviews* of employees, I have performance reviews of my slave. I don't want any Protocol included in our lives that my slave cannot follow.

Protocol Review

These policies and procedures will be reviewed and revised periodically, as Master directs. Master will consider a request for protocol review initiated by the slave.

While the slave may suggest additions, deletions or modification to any part of this document, such suggestions should be presented for Master's consideration in written form.

> **Commentary:** I feel strongly that every word in the Manual of Protocol (this book) is to be followed as it's listed. If we're not going to follow it, I want it removed from the Manual. If the slave would prefer to enact some protocol differently than I've described it, then I want to discuss this difference with the slave and decide whether I care enough about the difference to enforce my way of doing it or will change the listed protocol to conform to the slave's preference. On a few occasions my slave has made recommendations that improved the efficiency of a Protocol.
>
> In the same way that I decline to practice a dance step or a martial arts sequence unless I know exactly how it should be performed, I don't want some sloppy imitation of a protocol to be undertaken by the slave.

Slave Review

Occasionally, Master will ask the slave how she is adapting to her slavery. She is encouraged to use these opportunities to express concerns, fears or anxieties.

If issues arise that could affect the slave's ability to serve, she will ask Master to schedule private time to discuss and resolve these concerns.

Chapter 2

Social Issues

Interacting with Leather Masters: Leather events

Initial meeting with a Leather Master

The slave will treat a Leather Master with the same respect and deference that the slave shows me.

The slave will **NEVER** speak to a Leather Master without specific permission or without prior introduction. When being introduced to a Leather Master, the slave will assume a submissive stance, eyes lowered.

The slave will **NOT** extend her hand or provide any other gesture of personal recognition. However, the slave will curtsy and remain in her default position ("on point"), one pace behind and to the right of Master in a Standing Present position.

If Master decides to introduce the Dom or Master to the slave, the slave will respond to the introduction thus: "Sir, this slave is honored to meet you, Sir."

> **Commentary:** This is the first time in this Manual/Book that the slave has had to say something to someone other than her Master.

> **KEY COMMENTARY:** One of the defining characteristics of the Leather Lifestyle concerns the "greeting rituals" between Leathermen and between Leathermen and submissives/slaves. When two Leathermen meet, the Leatherman of highest rank extends his hand to the junior. Often, there is a pregnant moment while the two Leathermen try to sort out who is senior.

One of the most disrespectful things a slave or submissive can do when greeting a Leatherman — whether or not a Leather Master — is to smile broadly and offer a handshake. When I witness this, I'm always shaken by the split-second look of disapproval on the Leatherman's face and the quick recovery as he turns to the neophyte couple and politely asks the man: "Permission to shake your submissive's hand?" The proper response is: "Master ABC, I'd like to introduce you to my submissive (or slave), wxy; wxy, this is Master ABC."

Ongoing contact with a Master

The slave will follow all personal and service protocols specified in this manual when interacting with a Master to whom the slave has been previously introduced.

> **Commentary:** "Master" is a Leather title; Dom is a Not-Leather title. In the Introduction, I mentioned that I would address Leather protocols and Not-Leather protocols separately.

Interacting with Doms

Relations with Doms who are not Leathemen are less formal. The slave will be courteous and respectful — but the slave will not speak to or carry on discussions with a Dom without Master's permission unless there is an established relationship well known to Master, or unless the Dom has approached me for such Permission and I have granted it.

The slave does NOT have permission to ask to speak with another Dom. The Dom must first ask me for permission to speak with my slave.

> **Commentary:** Unlike the easy social communications that can go on in the "Vanilla" world (the non-kink world) with a spouse at a party or at some other social event, relations between your slave and Others involve a different frame of mind. When you think of another Master or Dom speaking with your slave, you might think of it as comparable to a person wanting to spend time with your particularly prized cat. On the one hand, you may be flattered that they are interested in your personal property, but on the other hand it may strike you as a little odd that they are interested in your personal property.

Physical Proximity when Others are Present

The slave will follow these rules when we are in High Protocol and in public:

- If Master is in private discussions with a Master or Dom, the slave will remove herself from within earshot but remain within eye contact.

- If the slave is approached by someone else during this time, this slave will inform that person that she is NOT free to speak, that she is Attending.

- The slave will not leave the position of Attending without instruction or permission to do so.

- In all other instances, the slave will maintain correct heeling position (on point).

Commentary: Although this may seem overly strict, these behaviors are necessary when other people are present so that Master can at any time communicate with his slave.

Service to Another Master, Dom or Vanilla Man

At times, the slave might have an opportunity to serve another Master or Dom. In such situations she will respect his protocols and rules as best she can, always remembering that she is bound to my rules and protocols by contract. They will at all times be respected.

If the other Master or Dom does not understand or respect the slave's existing obligations, she will dutifully inform him/her that she is not permitted to comply with his/her wishes. If there is any problem, she will inform Master at once in person or by phone. She will be VERY CAREFUL not to bring disrespect to our Family.

If email correspondence occurs, I am to receive a courtesy "CC" (courtesy copy — visible to the other person) so I can remain fully informed of this other relationship with my slave. When there are private meetings between my slave and another Master, Dom or Vanilla man, I expect a general briefing. I will not pry into details of a relationship that I have previously approved.

Commentary: Sometimes I may ask an established Master to take my slave for a weekend for specialized training. While the details will have been worked out between the other Master and me, my slave must understand that my basic rules and Instructions take precedence, and that she must bring Honor to our Household through her behavior.

Socializing in Public

Leathermen and Leatherwomen (Leatherfolk) are often referred to as a *Tribe*. The slave's relations with Tribe members will be different from the slave's relations with Doms from the Not-Leather BDSM community.

Relations in a Leather setting

By a "Leather setting," I mean an event, whether local or regional, that is presented for Leatherfolk. This could be a fairly informal Leather club meeting, an evening spent at a Leather bar, or a regional Leather conference.

In these settings, it is my intent that Leatherfolk will understand our Protocols and Symbols and will respect my slave's position within our Family.

Under NO CIRCUMSTANCES will this slave touch a Leather Master or a Leatherman. This is a serious sign of *disrespect* and will result in Correction.

In the presence of Leatherfolk, Masters shall be awarded the respect of their positions. The slave will refer to them by the honorific by which they are introduced, and afforded the courtesy given to a Master.

Subs will be acknowledged as such and the slave may converse casually with them, in the appropriate setting. **It is NOT appropriate to converse casually with a submissive or another slave while in active service to Master or when a scene is taking place.**

In the event that a Leatherman endeavors to hug my slave but this person *has not negotiated with me* for permission, the slave will be gracious and tactful, careful to avoid publicly embarrassing this person. If this situation occurs out of Master's sight — or occurs a second time — the slave will inform the novice Leatherman that she is in Protocol and — with respect — she does not have permission to return the hug. The slave will stand still and report the incident promptly.

> **Commentary:** This issue comes up occasionally in Austin because we're a "huggy" community. No offense is intended. Leatherfolk will ask: "Permission to hug?" before offering the hug, and a slave's Master will give "the nod." However, the protocols in this section govern the behavior I expect from my slave when we're in a more formal Leather setting.

Use of Furniture
In our home, in private, the slave is permitted to use furniture unless directed not to.

When attending an event in High Protocol the slave will not use furniture unless specifically directed to do so. If the use of furniture is necessary for some medical reason, the slave will inform me in private, preferably before the situation presents itself.

> **Commentary:** My sense is that the use/non-use of furniture is more of an issue in the Not-Leather community than in the world of Leather. Nonetheless, it is a powerful indicator of relative status. But at this writing I'm 62 and my slave is 51, so requiring her to sit on the floor strikes me as more severe than necessary in private. The slave knows that she is my property whether she is curled up at my feet or sitting next to me. And if there is some question about that, shame on me.

Relations in a Not-Leather BDSM Setting
Hugging: The slave is free to hug any other submissive *if and only if* she has asked Master to negotiate with that submissive's Dom either for initial or for ongoing permission to hug this Dom's submissive.

The slave is free to accept a hug from any Dom whom she KNOWS has negotiated that ongoing permission with me. In other cases, the slave will inform the Dom endeavoring to hug her that he must first obtain such permission from her Master.

Speaking: If Master indicates we are in High Protocol, the slave may not converse in public. If someone approaches the slave, she will lower her eyes and say: "Sir/Ma'am: this slave is in High Protocol tonight and may not speak."

> **Commentary:** Once again, these speaking, greeting and hugging protocols communicate the M/s dynamic within the Leather environment. These kinds of protocols keep the relationship up-front both in the Master's and in the slave's minds — and broadcast it to those nearby. Interestingly, this is also a way to share the celebration of one another with other Leatherfolk.

Special Situations

Being Loaned Out Overnight
In rare instances, the slave may be loaned out to another Dom or Master to learn a skill or for some practical service. Special rules govern the slave at these times.

- All activity expected of the slave will be pre-negotiated between Master and the person to whom the slave is being loaned (hereinafter: Host).

- Master will know the physical location where the slave is or will be. This assumes that the slave has been loaned to someone well-known to Master. If the person is *not well-known*, then standard safe call rules apply. (See Appendix B for discussion of the safe call process.

- If sexual intercourse is involved, this MUST be pre-negotiated with me and condoms must be used.

- For other play, the slave must not be marked.

The slave will phone Master when she arrives at the destination and will telephone Master precisely at 9 a.m. each morning while on loan.

If the slave is spending multiple days/nights on loan, she will also check in with Master precisely at noon and in the evening before 9 p.m. (at the convenience of the slave's Host). [Intent: not to require the slave to make an evening phone call that might interrupt the flow of evening activities.]

When speaking with Master in these situations, the slave will use the following communications code:

1. Emergency and call the police;

2. Emergency, come get me as soon as you can;

3. Not an emergency, but I don't feel comfortable. Please ask the Host to release me now. I can get home on my own;

4. No problem but not a very interesting experience — I'll stick it out;

5. Good experience, I'm having a nice time and hope to be loaned out to this person again.

Commentary: Readers familiar with the use of "safe calls" will immediately realize that some form of coded message must be used. For any readers not familiar with safe calls, the issue is that if the person is being held against his or her will and threatened, you cannot simply ask: "Hey, howyadoen out there? Feelin safe?" With a gun to his/her head, the answer will always be: "Oh, sure. No problem, I'm just fine. He's a great guy. No need for me to call you again."

So, when I receive the check-in call, I would open with: "Good morning, did you remember to take your pills?" The slave's answer will be: "Yes, Master, I took all five, thank you," indicating that everything is OK. I wouldn't start "chatting" until I had the number. This way, if it's a "one" I don't need to hear any more and the slave had the opportunity to get it out.

I take this coded message system **extremely seriously** and my slave and I always review it carefully before she is loaned out.

Reminders
The slave will write a formal "thank you" note to the Host within 24 hours after the visit. As usual, Master will be "copied" on all emails.

The slave does not have *prima facae* permission to maintain contact, either telephonic or email, with the Host. Permission for the Host to speak or write to the slave must be sought by the Host from Master. If the Host contacts the slave without permission, the slave will communicate that she does not have permission to speak or to write without such permission and that it is up to this person to ask Master whether she may respond.

Relations with Family and Friends

The slave may maintain her family relationships and will inform Master if she believes an order in some way limits her family contact. She will keep me apprised of family-related scheduling issues.

Minor children should not be made aware of the slave's status. Uninvolved adults should not be made fully aware of the slave's status. The slave is encouraged to maintain friendships with people who are aware of, and generally approve of, our lifestyle.

> **Commentary:** Whenever I enthusiastically describe my M/s relationship with my slave to someone outside our Community, I get the sense that I shouldn't have said anything. So, over the years, I say less and less to Outsiders.

Outside Friendships

The slave is specifically encouraged to develop and maintain friendships with others, whether male, female, Dom, slave or submissive. She will advise Master when she has opportunities to interact with others so that time for this activity can be allotted, if possible.

Occasionally, the slave may ask to host friends for an in-house function. If allowed, the slave may host the event, taking care to protect our property and privacy. The slave is responsible for the conduct of guests and for returning the house to an orderly state.

The slave may be permitted to spend time with acquaintances including dinners, movie outings, camping, etc. At Master's pleasure, these occasions may range from hours to several days in duration. The slave remains "on duty" during these occasions, remaining in full compliance with our contract and all protocols pertaining to personal behavior, dress and activities.

Commentary: Once again, the slave is valuable property. Master has invested a great deal of time, trouble and expense in training this slave. Master is always concerned with the quality and quantity of experiences to which the slave is exposed. The slave is always to be sensitive to her unusual status; these protocols reinforce that difference.

An M/s Studies Book

Chapter 3

Seamless Integration of Concept to Action

Standing Orders

Chain of Command
The slave serves Master. All decisions are made in this light. The only exceptions concern workplace demands placed on my slave, or certain critical issues that involve my slave's biological family.

Levels of Protocol
We will use no level of protocol around minors. For all other times there are three levels of protocol; each builds upon the other:

- **Social Protocol.** The slave refers to Master as "Master" or "Sir" but has no other language restriction. The slave is free to speak and ask questions without limitation. The slave may walk *almost* next to Master and in all other ways appear to be part of a "vanilla" couple.

- **Low Protocol.** Low Protocol is used when out in public (as in a mall or at a restaurant). Walking and standing protocols are invoked. The slave will not sit until Master has been seated. The slave will ask permission if she needs to go somewhere out of eyesight.

- **High Protocol.** All formal protocols are invoked — especially the *languaging* and *attending* protocols. The slave's sole purpose is to please me and make my life easier; the slave is *not* free to engage in discourse. The slave is expected to remain *highly alert* to any logistical issue or problem that may need to be solved (such as reminding me of someone's name or taking a business card being offered to me from another person).

Commentary: Because my formal Protocols are so complex and require practice, I use them every time my slave and I are together for dinner. That is, for the period up to dinner, we are either in low or in social protocol. But once we've showered and dressed for dinner (more on this, later) we conduct our "recommitment" ceremony and from that point until we go to bed, we're in High Leather Protocol.

Accessibility

The slave will be accessible by phone at all times. The slave will leave the cell phone turned on at ALL TIMES, including while charging. The slave is to be sure her cell phone is within her hearing even in her own home and is to carry the cell phone even when Master and the slave are out together, as previously referenced.

Any change in this arrangement, even for a few hours, requires Permission.

Commentary: The "cell phone issue" is another example that may appear overly strict. I can only say that this protocol has been worded this way to fit the way I am and the way I require my slave to be.

Agreements

For "things that matter," Master operates in the world of structured Agreements. Agreements have four components:

- State the offer/acceptance; (I agree…)
- Specify the general item to be done; (…to wash the outside of the car…)
- List conditions of satisfaction — be clear about the level of activity; (…so that all the dirt and tar are completely removed and no water spots remain…)
- Specify the time frame; (…within the next two hours.).

If the slave suspects that she cannot fully accomplish any of the four aspects of the Agreement, she must not agree to it; she must explain her reticence. The modification of any aspect of the Agreement **must** be done BEFORE the agreement is accepted or as soon as the need for modification becomes apparent.

If the slave has made an Agreement and discovers that she may be unable to complete it on time, she will contact Master and discuss the situation before the time period expires.

Failure to keep an Agreement will carry Consequences.

> **Commentary:** In my world, Agreements are a big deal. I don't use them casually. I don't mind modifying an agreement on the front end; I don't even mind being contacted regarding a change to the deadline. However, I mind a great deal if no effort was made to renegotiate the terms and conditions of an Agreement and it is not fulfilled exactly as it was set.
>
> Because I am so focused on keeping Agreements perfectly, I caution my slave not to enter lightly into a formal Agreement with me. I'm going to be easier to get along with if the slave says: "Master, I cannot fulfill the terms you are proposing" rather than entering into the Agreement suspecting that the terms cannot be fulfilled.
>
> I will comment further on this point. I've known people who would agree to do about anything with little or no intention of doing so. I knew a professor who would promise anything just to get you to go away. While it seemed that he was being cooperative and helpful he was simply manipulative. His behavior was passive-aggressive. Aware of my personal sensitivity to this point — that I will aggressively challenge any failure to keep an Agreement — I explain it to those who work closely with me. Similarly, on those occasions that I feel an Agreement is needed to accomplish some significant Task, I'm careful to review the component parts of an Agreement and remind the slave of the importance of communicating changes to me **ahead of time**.

Time Commitments

In this Household, issues of *time* are important. *Time commitments* represent a daily opportunity to keep your word. They are a form of Agreement.

If the slave has been told an arrival or departure time, Master expects that time to be honored to the second. There will be Consequences to violating time issues.

Commentary: "Keeping one's word" is a core concept within the Leather culture. From the very beginning of my exposure to the Leather World, I was struck by the degree of honesty, integrity and high moral purpose I found there. If a Leatherman says something will be done, you can be sure it will be. If I, as Master, have told someone that I will arrive at a certain time, tardiness by my slave will NOT cause me to be late to that meeting. If my slave is not ready to leave on time, I will leave without her and attend to her Consequences later.

Health and Hygiene

Master may permanently mark or modify the slave's body to suit our purposes.

- The slave will maintain her body in a manner that ensures her good health and our enjoyment of her body. Specifically, the slave will keep her weight reasonably proportional to her height and build. Pursuant to that, the slave will exercise according to specific Instructions provided at Master's pleasure.

- The slave will attempt to avoid disease. Should medical or dental attention be required, the slave will advise Master and promptly seek appropriate care. The slave will have annual physical, dental, and gynecological exams.

- The slave will ensure that the hair on her head is neatly combed and styled in a manner that Master has approved. She will also maintain her fingernails and toenails in a feminine and artistic manner.

- The slave will shave her pubic hair daily.

Commentary: This section is pretty straightforward. As the Master is responsible for the slave's physical well-being, topics in this section are really pro forma. Said differently, Master is ensuring that his property remains in good, clean working order so as to be of maximum use and availability. In addition, other than having manicures and pedicures, I do not require anything of my slave that I do not exact upon myself.

Issues of Communication

Courtesies and conversations often rely on *tact*. *Tact* is the talent for not saying that you were right in the first place. In our Family, we are not interested in affixing *blame,* we are interested in developing rich, harmonious relationships. The relevant aphorism is: "We're not put on this earth to see through one another, but to see one another through."

Silent Hand Signals

When we are in public, it often occurs that I need to communicate with the slave. If we are alone, it's easy enough simply to tell the slave what I wish; however, if others are around or if we are in a Leather setting, it is often more pleasing to communicate silently to the slave. To avoid confusion, I use only a few silent signals.

STOP or SILENCE: If we are walking and I bring my closed fist up to shoulder height, close to the body, the slave knows to stop immediately (as opposed to running into me). If we are already stopped and for some reason I wish the slave either to stop speaking or not to start speaking, I use the same signal.

Come to me or I want to say something to you: When entertaining Others or when out in public (whether or not it is a Leather event), the slave always keeps me in view. By placing the first and second fingers of my right hand on the muscle of my left upper-arm, the slave knows immediately to attend me.

Commentary: Much of the mystery and magic that accompanies an M/s couple in public concerns their dance, the effortless way they move together. Part of the magic is created through the use of silent gestures. Here, I've only touched on a few basic gestures; I'll describe more when we get to the section about how to present. Some people scene through their whips or their floggers. We scene through our protocols, every time we are together.

Conversation Conventions in this Family

In our Family, there are three overriding principles when non-Family members are present:

- First: don't correct a Family member in public. All corrections are conducted in private. Violation of this Protocol will have dramatic consequences, because it communicates disharmony and lack of respect.

- Second: "It's better to be interested than interesting." Don't go on at length about how much you know or where you've been in the world.

- Third: Humility is a good thing. We all have plenty to be humble about.

Commentary: In conversations, we make a point of supporting people, not demonstrating how clever we can be. No one likes to be "outshone" in public; no one likes to be corrected in public. Such actions display personal insecurity as well as discourtesy towards others. Worse, if directed towards a Family member, it risks displaying disunity within the Family. Apart from all that, it undermines relationships and demonstrates poor manners.

Direct Questions from Another

When the slave doesn't know the answer to a direct question…:

- Admit it. No one is expected to know everything. The slave will gain more "points" for admitting they don't know something than in trying to concoct or guess at the answer.

- Find out the answer and tell the person. The form of response, here, is: "Sir, I don't know the answer, Sir, but I will find out and tell you."

- She must stand by her Word and complete this "loop;" she must live in her Integrity.

When the slave DOES know the answer to a direct question but the slave fears that the person asking the question won't like the answer, then consider the following:

- First, is this "small talk" to keep the conversation going, or is it a serious "content" discussion? If small talk, providing a refined or more accurate correction might kill the mood. If it is a serious discussion and the speaker is not being precise or accurate, the slave will have to weigh the consequences of "being right" by providing better information.

- For our Family purposes, my preferred "transition phrase" in this kind of situation is: "It seems to me I read somewhere…" then give the correct answer. This leaves open the possibility that the slave may not be remembering the fact exactly. It softens the blow.

Commentary: While people are generally driven to please and to give answers that please, my experience is that one gains more "personal points" for admitting they **don't know something** and providing the answer later, if at all. In like manner, I have found that there are **often** times when it's FAR BETTER to avoid providing better or more complete explanations about a discussion topic, as the less informed person dislikes being shown up in public. This is one area in which my slave's skills exceed my own.

Jokes: The slave will be wary of jokes. Master is VERY sensitive about jokes. In our Family, there will be **NO** jokes where a person or sub-culture is the subject or where a person's condition (being Polish, Jewish, Blond, poor, dumb…) is ridiculed. Personal stories are not considered to be jokes.

Taboo Subjects: The well-known Three: religion, race, and politics plus topics such as: death, disasters, accidents, serious illness and — with Elders present — their age or mine.

Conversational Ease

Everyone associated with this Family is expected to speak grammatically correct English and to strive to build a large and rich vocabulary.

To be a good conversationalist, one must first have something to say. Second, one must be able to say it well. To achieve the first goal — having something to say — members of this Family are expected to have personal areas of competence and to maintain at least a passing familiarity with current events. Poor grammar and/or the use of a simple vocabulary seriously inhibit one's ability to communicate effectively. Words communicate concepts. An advanced vocabulary improves one's ability to communicate and understand complex ideas.

> **Commentary:** These Protocols fit my background and preferences. They may not fit other M/s couples. I spend a great deal of my time around highly educated people. They are susceptible to judging negatively people with poor grammar and simple vocabulary. While I certainly don't want my slave to behave pretentiously, neither do I want her to leave the impression that she is poorly educated or unwilling to learn to use her native language with accuracy and lucidity.
>
> It is almost as important that my slave be capable of demonstrating our interest in people's ideas by asking intelligent questions, thought-provoking questions that draw others into discourse. Her grammar and vocabulary should contribute to the conversation, demonstrating our high regard for those whose company we enjoy, rather than distracting from it by jarring the senses (like discordant music).
>
> When our company feels flattered by our interest, it builds camaraderie, encourages people to include us in further rich and stimulating discussion. When my slave can contribute interesting questions to a conversation, not only can it benefit me by broadening my experience, but can also minimize the discomfort I sometimes feel when conversations are reduced to banalities and small talk.
>
> In our personal case, my slave and I frequently exercise our "vocabulary kink" in the evenings by pouring over the Oxford

English Dictionary, happily chasing down one rabbit trail after another in this fifteen-volume set of dictionaries that weigh about seven pounds each. At this writing, we are reading the Dictionary of Differences (Parragon Books, 1993) during our evening meal. Here, we explore and discuss differences between such words as: decry/descry, pore/pour, and tortuous/torturous.

Honesty in Verbal Communication

It is critical that all Family Members be honest and direct in all their dealings.

One can avoid a great deal of embarrassment by giving precise answers to questions asked by Seniors (the term used in the Leather Community for a Leatherman more experienced than the slave). If the slave cannot give a complete or correct answer, then she is to answer only as much of the question as possible without being misleading or evasive. It is always appropriate to say: "This slave doesn't know, Sir (or Ma'am), but she will find out and let you know." If the slave offers this response, be sure to write a note that the slave now owes this person an answer. When the slave takes on an Obligation of this sort, she would do well to inform Master of the exchange *in writing*.

> **Commentary:** The last sentence is important. If the slave intends to take on an Obligation **not assigned by Master**, the slave **must** inform Master about it. Failure to do so is willful and against the spirit of the M/s dynamic. Because I tend to forget easily, I write notes about everything. If the slave gives me a note, I can easily file it electronically so that I keep track of the issue. If the slave tells me of something she intends to do, I am likely to forget the conversation ever took place.

Rank and Respect

While the senior may rarely think of it when speaking with a junior (again, the term used in the Leather Community for the less senior Leatherperson), the junior will never forget their difference in rank. This is as it should be. Understanding this maxim should make it easy to speak respectfully with those of different standing within our Community; violation may bring embarrassment.

Courtesies to Juniors

Those associated with our Family will exhibit the utmost courtesy and caring aid to juniors, particularly juniors who are invited to one of our Dining Experiences. They will be made to feel welcomed and honored. Any discourtesy towards others reflects poorly on the Honor and Integrity of the Family and will be viewed in that light.

Conflict in Conversations

The occasion may arise when someone states an opinion that substantially opposes the slave's opinion. Unless some action is called for on the slave's part, she is to ignore the comment out of respect for the senior's greater age or experience. If the slave is asked for her specific opinion on this matter and cannot avoid answering, the form of reply is: "With due respect, Sir, in this matter of opinion my experience has been to the contrary." Then, she may voice her opinion.

Apologies for Social Gaffes

If the slave has harmed or hurt someone needlessly or through carelessness, the slave must do more than apologize; she must ask this person's forgiveness. If the slave fails to keep an appointment, she must telephone, email or write a brief note explaining her failure to do so — and the reason must be a good one.

In a High Protocol setting, if the slave is asked by a Dom or Master to carry out some non-trivial request, the proper response is: "Sir, that question must be asked of Master; this slave does not have the authority to grant you such a request."

If the slave breaks or damages something, the slave will try to replace the article exactly. If this is not possible, the slave will then send flowers or a book of interest to the person with a note saying she is sorry for the mishap.

In a non-Leather setting, if the slave steps or passes in front of someone, or bumps into them, the slave will say: "Please excuse me" or "I beg your pardon." In High Protocol, the slave will say: "Sir, please excuse this slave's clumsiness" or "This slave apologizes for having bumped you, Sir."

Commentary: Again, the slave represents the Master and our "social IQ" will be transmitted through her social circle like wildfire, whether in a "Vanilla" or "Leather" setting. I ask nothing of my slave that I do not do myself.

Behavior in Public

This set of protocols establishes a *way of being* in the world both for the Master and the slave. These protocols help to affirm Master's expectation that the slave will always be available and attentive when they are together. Because the Master walks with another person shadowing his/her footsteps, some rules have to be established about how this "shadow-person" moves and behaves. If the slave is to *serve* Master and *not be a burden* to Master, the slave must know how to keep out of the way and how to be helpful.

Standing

Any time the slave is in public with Master, the slave will assume her position "on point." That is, she will maintain Public Present position ("parade rest") slightly behind Master's right shoulder. So long as Master is standing, the slave will remain standing in that physical location. If Master wishes the slave to come around to a position facing him, he will either instruct her to move into his range of vision or use the Family's silent hand signal to cause her to change positions (two fingers of my left hand on my right forearm).

If the slave is seated on a chair or on the floor, the slave will stand whenever Master enters or leaves the same room or space — unless Master waives this protocol by an immediate order to "sit," "stay," or "continue."

Sitting

It is my wish that the slave sit on furniture unless High Protocol is invoked, in which case the slave will not sit on any furniture without a direct and specific order by Master.

When seated and not eating at Table, the slave's hands should be in her lap, knees together, feet positioned demurely to the side, ankles crossed.

Walking

The slave normally walks in a position that I refer to as "on point." That is, to the right and about one step behind Master. The slave is to assume a position that is natural yet reflects our respective rank. The slave is to be near enough that Master can easily speak with her and give her Orders.

Eating

While I have provided much more detail later in this book (in the *dining rituals* section), in summary, the protocols are as follows:

- Master will seat the slave at the table; under no circumstances will the slave seat herself unless Master has directed this action.

- Once seated, the slave will sit motionless until Master completes the "centering" ceremony. Note: If we are sitting in a booth rather than in chairs this step is omitted.

- Once Master is seated, the slave will wait until Master removes his napkin before removing her napkin from the table and placing it folded in half on her lap (crease towards her body).

- If this is an evening meal with cocktails or wine, the slave will wait until Master has offered the first toast before sipping.

- The slave will not eat a morsel of food from any course of the meal until Master has first taken a bite and then fed a single bite to the slave, who will proceed to eat at a pace that Master sets. When Master places his fork and knife across his plate to signal that he has finished eating, the slave will do the same regardless of any food left on her plate.

- The slave will closely monitor all beverages Master is drinking and ensure that they are kept filled without prompting.

Commentary: I try to bring ceremony into daily life. I wish to celebrate as many aspects of Life as possible, to recognize even the ordinary and commonplace aspects as special. Dining offers many opportunities to do so.

Doors and Elevators

The slave will open doors and elevators (and any related apparatus) for Master and will follow once I have passed through. In the case of elevators, the slave will enter after all others and then press the elevator buttons, as needed. The slave will remain in the elevator, holding the door until Master and his party (if any) have exited.

In the case of door configurations where there is an outer and inner door, the slave will open the first door to let Master pass, then enter and — as Master waits — open the second door.

Should a third person be present with us, we will discuss door protocols beforehand, but the general concept is that the slave is Master's *Personal Assistant* and must remain "attached" to Master at all times. Thus, if the slave is holding a door, the slave will enter after Master and turn any remaining "door holding" duties over to the third.

When the Third is part of the Leather Lifestyle and is Senior to me, my slave will continue to hold the door until that person has passed through.

When the Third is part of the Leather Lifestyle and acts as the junior slave when with us, s/he will be expected to move ahead of my slave to open and hold a door or elevator until both my slave and I have passed through.

> **Commentary:** This may sound complicated, but it is not. These door-handling protocols arise all the time when we are at Leather conferences.

Driving

When Master is driving: Despite the more common Master/slave dynamic, it is my wish that the slave not enter or leave a vehicle on her own. Master will open the door in order for the slave to enter or exit the car.

When the slave is driving: There are times when the slave will serve Master as *chauffeur* (discussed later). In those instances, the above-stated protocol is reversed and the slave will open the door for Master to enter and exit the passenger side of the car.

Commentary: Increasingly, as our M/s dynamic evolves, my slave serves as chauffeur. As you will read later, she is dressed entirely in black (including black blazer) and wears a chauffeur's cap when fulfilling this role. We do this in order to have fun and to indulge in some roleplay and fetish dressing.

Handshakes

Leather Protocol calls for personal reserve. Despite the culture of southern hospitality and genteel upbringing in which the slave was raised, under no circumstances will this slave extend a hand to a Dom unless the slave knows that such a gesture has been pre-negotiated and approved.

If the slave DOES have permission to shake hands or to hug another Dom/Master, this slave will attend to the length of such contact. Contact must be socially appropriate in order not to be misinterpreted as a "forward" gesture.

When a submissive in our Family shakes hands with (or hugs) another submissive, the less senior, or if this is unknown, the *younger or less experienced submissive* waits for the older or higher ranking submissive to extend his/her hand in greeting.

Junior submissives *rise* to greet more senior submissives.

In Low Protocol and Social Protocol settings, the slave is to follow polite southern gestures of hospitality.

Commentary: The action of a slave extending her hand to a Dom, Leatherman or Leather Master in a Leather setting is a huge breach of protocol within the community.

Introductions

The less senior Leatherman is always presented to the more senior Leatherman. "Master Steve, may I present George?"

Even in settings that are not Leather, avoid automatically introducing a Dom to another Dom's submissive or slave. When such introduction is required the Host Dom will ask the Dom responsible for the submissive/

slave to make the introduction, thus: "George, may I ask you to present William to your slave?"

If the host Dom is not immediately available, a Dom seeking an introduction may address the submissive's Dom, thus: "George, would you be kind enough to introduce me to your slave/submissive?"

When making a presentation, the name of the higher ranked Dom is always spoken first.

> **Commentary:** There are regional differences in protocols used within the BDSM community in the U.S. I can only write from my experience that there is no particular expectation that a Dom who is not in a Leather setting will feel the slightest inclination to introduce his submissive to another Dom. In Leather settings there is more formality and more formal courtesy (and less perceived threat of competition); Masters almost always introduce their slaves when in social settings.

Forms of Address

Following the guidelines set forth in the Butchmann's protocols, my slave will address me as "Master" or "Sir" in every sentence uttered (e.g.: "Master, permission to leave the room?"). Others who are associated with the Family in submissive positions but *not* as slaves will address me as "Sir." Those associated with the Family will address other Doms or Masters as "Sir" unless the individual is a recognized Leather Master, in which case the honorific "Master" will be used along with the person's name (e.g.: Master Skip or Master Steve).

The slave has no reason to speak to any Master, Leatherman or Dom who has not been formally introduced to her. Thus, the slave should already know whether the person is a Leather Master or not.

> **Commentary:** Only my slave may call me "Master." It is a title reserved for her, alone.

Speaking in Public – Social or Leather Event

If the slave has something to communicate to Master, the slave will move into Master's range of vision and **wait to be recognized.** The slave is **not** to speak until recognized unless responding to Master's questions, or until the slave has been invited to participate in an ongoing conversation. Once a conversation is started, the slave is free to speak until that conversation ends, at which point the process repeats.

Commentary: This is another example of the kind of protocol that can vary between Owners. For example, the strict view is that speaking in public *of her own free will* is not permitted. A different Owner may wish the his or her slave to behave differently on this point.

My slave sometimes bristles at the restraints I place on her. She is well read, extremely high IQ and alive with questions and observations. Nonetheless, I am fairly reclusive and frequently prefer silence. In our M/s Relationship, we have worked out a code whereby she can speak with me when she has something important to say on occasions when I prefer silence.

Serving

When serving food or drinks, the slave will follow the concept of *sprezzatura* (effortless technique), previously discussed. The relevant protocols are:

- Approach slowly and with grace. DO NOT APPEAR HURRIED or harrowed.

- Hold a plate with both hands underneath;

- Hold a long stemmed wine glass with base resting on left hand and with right hand stabilizing the stem of the glass;

- Hold a coffee mug or glass of liquid (**filled only ¾ full**) by placing it directly on the slave's left or right hand, half of the mug on the fingers, half on the palm of the hand, the other hand holding up the hand that holds the mug. The slave is forbidden to stabilize the coffee mug in any other way;

- Hold a cup and saucer in the same fashion.

- Should any liquid be spilled, the slave is to remove the food/liquid, clean the spill and start over from the beginning.

- Before handing the food/beverage to Master, the slave will assume a "full present" position and, with deliberation, kiss the edge of the plate/glass/mug/cup with eyes lowered. The slave will then look up into Master's eyes and present the gift with a slow and deliberate gesture. Note: the *intent*, here, is that the slave **focus** her attention on the moment; that the slave demonstrate cognizance of her status and the importance of the ceremony of *service.*

- The slave will then rise to a standing position in one single, fluid motion and without having to stabilize herself in the process. That is, the slave will roll back from a kneeling position to a squatting position with both knees together and then use the legs to rise to a standing position. There will be no "jerkiness" in this action. (Note: The secret is to use the weight of the head to provide stability.)

- The slave will then stand for the count of three (demonstrating *intentionality)*, curtsy, take three small steps backward, turn and leave. Note: The slave will **not** turn her back on Master prior to taking three backward steps.

Commentary: This Protocol is about being present during serving rituals. As service is one of the core concepts of M/s relations; **how** that service is rendered becomes an Issue. I am extremely "present" with my slave. I pay attention to her every move and revel in its perfection. I would never ignore her efforts by not being present.

Communication

Timely and Relevant
My slave will contact me in a timely manner by phone and/or email to express needs or to report on anything relevant to my life. I prefer not to be told of events or issues that are not germane to our relationship. If the slave can "manage" or "handle" a situation without involving me, she should do so.

Commentary: Life is complicated and busy enough without the slave adding to it with unrelated issues/concerns. The slave's role is to remove problems from my life, not to add problems. Since small issues can grow larger if not caught early, timeliness in communication is important.

Expressing Dissatisfaction

Pre-topic commentary: What follows is a discussion of the slave's **attitude**. Let's be real about this: my slave is a vibrant woman with profound feelings. For this relationship to work, it must be fulfilling to both parties. If the slave is unhappy, Master will be unhappy (later). It's important that the slave communicate appropriately any unhappiness at receiving an Order or Instruction.

Should the slave feel the need to express that her feelings are hurt or that she is being overtaxed in some way, the slave is instructed to communicate these sentiments in an appropriate manner as soon as they are recognized.

- "Appropriate manner" can be: "Master, with respect, I'm feeling Overburdened with this Task: may I explain my current workload?"

- "Master, when you… I feel… because…" (Note: this is my preferred formula for communicating an emotional issue.)

If an *extreme emotional hurt* occurs, our Contract calls for a particular protocol. Because this is specified in our Contract, it takes precedence over anything written in this Protocol Manual. My slave will assume the status of her non-slave self (name withheld for privacy reasons) and use My given name: "Bob…" My slave *never* uses My given name, so the world stops while she and Bob sort out what happened and how to fix it. (P.S.: It's usually My fault, except that Masters are never wrong, right?)

Commentary: In my view, most interpersonal issues/problems arise among couples — whether in Vanilla or BDSM relationships — because the couple (usually the man) lacks the skills to maneuver around and through emotional upsets. This is a case where the more counseling/therapy and study the Master has put into learning how to understand and how to work with Others, the better the chance that the M/s relationship will survive. I know a number of men who have tried M/s relationships over and over and over and just can't quite figure out why they don't work. The answer, in my opinion, is that these Doms lack the interpersonal skills to build solid, nurturing, long-term relationships whether in the "Vanilla" or the Kink world.

In my view, it all rests in each member of the couple being willing to admit that they can be wrong, usually about an emotional attitude.

Apologies

"Sir, I beg your pardon, Sir" is how the slave expresses regret for an accidental mishap. A slave would not say "Sorry" or "Excuse me," as these forms imply that the slave acted of her own will. Such statements are contrary to the core tenants of a Master/slave relationship.

Commentary: The more you study M/s relations and the more you work with a slave, the more you understand the importance of getting the slave to understand thoroughly that a slave has no free will; that the slave is serving YOUR will exclusively. The rare times that my slave gets in Trouble with me, she has taken an initiative during a time when I gave her a time-sensitive Task. That is: after specific discussions, I thought that my slave was going to do "X" over the lunch hour and the next thing I know she's done "Y" without re-negotiating the deal. This is seriously "not-OK" with me and leads to immediate Consequences.

Oral Communications

When we are in *social* or *high* protocol, the slave will use the words "Master" or "Sir" in every sentence. My *request* is that this protocol is always followed, regardless of the social setting or stated protocol level.

Commentary: This is one of the Protocols that you must practice to avoid confusion when you change from the lowest protocol level to a higher level. To avoid confusing situations, we've found it easier always to use this Protocol.

Written Communications

The Protocol for written communications is as follows:

- The slave opens the communication with "Master;"

- Capitalizes the first letter in any reference to me (e.g.: "You, Your" etc.);

- Uses lowercase in any reference to herself (e.g.: "i"); and

- Closes with a lowercase name in the last sentence.

Email Communications with Others

The slave will copy Master when writing to ANY Dom/Domme or Leatherman. The slave must have Permission to initiate and/or to maintain such communication.

Commentary: We are a polyamorous Family. I encourage contact between my slave and Others. However, I must know about these relationships; I must be comfortable that my property is at no risk of psychological or physical damage and one way of monitoring the slave's well-being is to monitor both sides of all correspondence. When this has occurred in the past, my slave has made it clear to the other person that he is to copy me on all email to her. As a matter of practice, I release the other man from this requirement after I have a sense of his honor and integrity and only require my slave to keep me generally apprised of the relationship.

How to Ask a Question

The proper form for questions regarding any possible action by the slave is, "Sir, do you wish this slave to [description of action], Sir?"

It is immaterial if the word "wish" is replaced with "want," "desire," "intend" and so on. It is also immaterial if the action is simple (like going to the bathroom or answering the phone) or complex (like getting ready to go out to theater), or a prelude to further conversation (asking if Master wishes the slave to tell him something). What matters is that instead of the slave expressing her own desire and asking Master to approve or reject it (an accidental regression to an earlier time in the slave's life, to be sure), the slave presents a possibility *without "investing herself" in it* and awaits Master's decision.

> **Commentary: Living in obedience** goes beyond doing only as you're told; it means that the slave also wants only what the slave's Master wants.

How to Make a Response

As Master's response to the slave's question is effectively an order, the slave's response to any order, Instruction, acknowledgement, correction, explanation, or information conveyed by Master is, "Sir, yes, Sir! Thank you, Sir!"

The same form is used whenever the slave answers a question in the affirmative. If the slave's answer is negative, then, "Sir, no, Sir! Thank you, Sir!"

Occasionally these forms may be varied by inserting "Master" ("Sir, yes, Sir! Thank you, Master!"), but the basic form is invariant — life can be wonderfully simple when almost everything calls for the same response!

> **Commentary:** In reality, while the slave has no trouble replying to every sentence with: "Yes, Master" or "Yes, Sir," I have found it more difficult in everyday life to get my slave to use this more formal structure. I have been lax in enforcing this, for I believe that in simplifying the response to "Yes, Sir", the slave fulfills the intent of the structure and that use of the more formal military wording is less important. Said differently, you have to pick your fights and this one strikes me as a trivial matter in the overall scheme of an M/s relationship.
>
> In High Protocol my slave is much better about remembering to use the two-Sir sentence construction.

Extended Questions or Comments – High Protocol

Invoked only in High Protocol, if the slave feels the need to ask an involved question or one that will require more than a yes/no response from Master, the slave asks, "Sir, do you wish your slave to ask a question, Sir?"

Similarly, in High Protocol, if the slave feels the need to make a comment, the slave asks, "Sir, do you wish your slave to make a comment, Sir?" In both cases, the slave awaits Master's response, and says, "Sir, yes, Sir! Thank you, Sir!" whether the response is affirmative or negative, and, finally, if the response was affirmative, asks her question or makes her comment (beginning each sentence with "Sir" as usual and ending the last sentence with "Sir" as well).

> **Commentary:** Each Master must decide how freely the slave is allowed to speak. The desire for the Relationship to last is at the core of the M/s dynamic. If both Master and slave are introverts, this formality may be seen as a godsend (because it cuts down on the idle chatter that neither party would desire). On the other hand, if both Master and the slave are extroverts, protocols that limit speech probably won't work. In my case, both my slave and I are "researchers" who would rather read than talk, so these restrictive protocols work well for us.

No Arguments

The slave is never wrong to ask for clarification of orders given to her or to offer to inform Master of something that troubles her — or, for that matter, brings the slave joy! Leading questions and argumentative expressions of opinion must be avoided. The slave is always to consider herself Master's property; a Being wholly devoted to fulfilling Master's will.

At Master's discretion, Master and the slave may discuss any matter at all — but they do not argue!

Chapter 4

"How to Be" in Master's Presence

Protocols when in Master's Presence

The Master/slave Relationship is a special one. The number of successful BDSM M/s Households in the world is miniscule. The Protocols in this section celebrate the unusual nature of this dynamic; they call both for the Master and the slave to come present to their Relationship.

Note: Most of the material in this chapter — especially the two sections *Presenting/Continuing* and *Refinements in the Art of Service* — are based upon the protocols developed by APEX Academy/Butchmann's. As the original material has been so interlaced with my comments and our adapted versions of the original, it is not practical to supply quotation marks around each quoted line, but know that this material is mostly from that source. Again, I thank Master Steve Sampson for permitting their use in this book.

Coming Present Before Beginning our Evening

"Coming together" after a day's absence (when the slave has to work) or coming together on a weekend evening when we have been out of protocol all day is marked by *ceremony.*

The slave will enter the house, find Master, and assume the *full present* position. I welcome the slave, and if I have something planned for the evening that requires special dress, I so inform her. This is NOT the time for our "recommitment ceremony," so after this brief greeting I take her hands and assist her in rising (this is not a time that I wish her to get up on her own), kiss her and send her on her way to attend to the house, shower and dress for dinner. The slave will now take about 45 minutes preparing herself for our Evening. [Note: Master will also dress and then retire to the living room to read while awaiting the slave's return. The slave will not interrupt before she finishes dressing.]

When the slave next appears, she will be Dressed (discussed in Chapter 5). This is now the start of our Evening and we are now in High Protocol.

The slave will seek out Master and assume the Gorean Nadu position (from the "Gor" novels). This command is slightly different from the Full Present used in the Leather world; I prefer the look of it.

In this position the slave kneels, her feet crossed behind her, and sits upon her heels with her back and shoulders straight, her chest out, belly in, and her head up, though she averts her eyes to the floor. Her thighs are open, widely spread, her hands rest upon her thighs palms upward.

The slave remains in this position until recognized.

Nadu is *principally* used when we conduct the ritual of our "Recommitment Ceremony," that generally follows this format:

The slave assumes the Nadu position:

1. Master: "What have we here?"
2. slave: "Your slave, Master"
3. Master: "So it is. And what in the world shall I do with a slave?"
4. slave: "Take me as Yours, if it Pleases You, Master."
5. Master: "And why should I do such a thing?"
6. slave: "Because You own me, Master, and because we love one another."
7. Master: "While those are both good reasons, it seems to me that the key question is 'Are you Willing?'" *
8. slave: "Yes, Master, i am Willing."
9. Master: "In that case, I Accept you. Please rise."

Upon Master's signal, slave rolls up (backwards) in one fluid motion to standing position.

* Yes, Master Steve, I pay attention to You.

Commentary: With very few exceptions, we go through this ritual daily, and have done so since she accepted my collar.

Coming Present after Being Together in Low Protocol All Day

Frequently on weeknights, but particularly on weekends, we will use "Dressing" as the point of demarcation between low protocol and the high protocol of our Evenings together. Master will inform the slave when to begin the bathing/changing process and the form of dress required for that evening. The "Recommitment Ceremony" follows once the slave has dressed.

Presenting/Continuing

In many M/s relationships, the ceremony of greeting and leaving is managed through "presenting." Here, the slave takes a specific position, pauses to feel her slavery, waits for Master to acknowledge her, announces her presence and readiness to obey, and, finally, waits to be given a specific order or told to "continue." All these aspects of presenting are described in further detail, below. This section provides a glimpse of how "presenting" often works in a high protocol setting.

Entering and Leaving Master's Presence and Control

Because of the special kind of relationship shared between Master and slave, Master has selected certain ritual reminders that help her focus and reflect on the reality of her status. For example, the slave will not say "Hello" to Master. As previously discussed, the slave is not a "girlfriend." When the slave greets Master, the slave is surrendering herself to Master's control. Therefore, the greeting must be Special.

Similarly, when the slave takes leave of Master, the slave is requesting that his control be extended beyond Master's direct presence. Therefore, casual, familiar greetings and farewells are replaced by disciplined, thoughtful processes and rituals.

When to Present

The slave is expected to present:

- When the slave comes into or leaves Master's presence; thus, at any time when under social conditions a "Hello" or "Goodbye" would be appropriate.

- When the slave needs to ask a question of Master or receive additional instructions to complete an assigned task.

- When the slave has completed all currently assigned tasks and awaits Master's pleasure. The slave who has finished her assigned tasks does not simply go off and do as the slave pleases when Master is present, but instead asks what Master desires her to do. (If Master is not present, the slave should follow her best judgment in light of the slave's training and standing orders.)

When another slave presents in the same space, my slave is never merely to watch another slave present, but is to join in the process by taking the present position (that is, without the verbal portion) and holds this position while awaiting her Master's order to "continue." This rule underscores that all slaves are brothers/sisters and equals who support each other's slavery in any way possible.

The complete presenting ritual is not required when Master or slave comes and goes repeatedly in the course of normal household or other activities. However, if seated, the slave will ordinarily stand whenever Master enters the space the slave occupies and remains in the Standing Present position until told to "sit" or "continue."

If the slave who has recently presented to Master re-enters Master's space before completing her duties then she should simply do her task as inconspicuously as possible and (once the task is completed) assume a standing present position until given further instructions.

How to Present
To the best of my knowledge, Leather tradition has the slave performing Formal Present (a kneeling position) in most situations. Because of our ages, it is my preference that my slave use the Standing Present as her default position both in public and in private.

By presenting, the slave brings herself within Master's awareness and waits for acknowledgement without disturbing whatever Master is doing. If it is Master who enters a space where the slave is engaged, the slave stops whatever she was doing and assumes a Standing Present to indicate that she is prepared to follow any direction Master wishes to give her.

Traditional Present positions. The following formal positions commonly used in the Leather tradition express the strength of the slave and the power of her obedience. With the exception of the Honor Present, all are held without moving until the slave is released by an order from the Master to whom the slave is presenting. The four positions may be modified in special circumstances (for instance, if the slave is on crutches or must use a wheelchair). When Master signals these positions the intent is to convey the message that we have moved into high protocol. This might occur in a public setting when we meet someone else from the Leather Tribe.

> **Full Present:** The slave kneels upright (on both knees, not sitting on her heels). Her knees are spread shoulder width apart, arms locked behind her back, each hand clasping the opposite forearm (or wrist if she is incapable of grasping the forearm); her chest is held forward, wide and strong; her head bowed with eyes down. This is the default form and normally used whenever Master is sitting or lying down. [Note: I prefer eye contact from my slave, not a "head lowered" position.]

I silently signal the slave to take this position by pointing my index finger towards the floor with two rapid downward motions.

Honor Present: The Honor Present is the same as the Full Present except only the right knee touches the ground and the left leg is bent. In either case, after the slave makes her greeting statement such as: "Sir, on behalf of my Master, I am honored to meet you." The slave stands again without waiting for a command. An Honor Present is used to greet a Leather Master or Guest — in public or in private — who might be embarrassed if the slave waits for an order to "continue."

I silently signal Honor Present by gesturing toward the floor with the flat of my hand, all fingers extended.

Standing Present calls for the slave to stand with legs shoulder-width apart, hands behind the back, each hand grasping the opposite forearm. This is used in private or in public Leather events as the default "attending" position.

I silently signal the "Standing Present" and "Public Present" positions by extending my right hand straight to my side and pointing the index finger of my right hand forward and horizontal to the floor (not AT the floor) and then rotating my wrist 90-degrees. The slave knows to perform the Standing Present when Master is standing and if we are in private or at a public Leather event. The slave knows I use the same hand signal to indicate *Public Present* when we are in public and we do not want to draw unwarranted attention to the kneeling position of a Full Present.

Public Present uses the same overall posture as "Standing Present," except that the hands are positioned in a manner that lets anyone behind the slave see her open palms held crossed behind the small of the slave's back, similar to a military "parade rest." As just mentioned, this is used in public when kneeling — or even the unusual arm positions of the Standing Present — might draw undesirable attention.

Commentary: While there may be other forms of Present and other hand signals used to invoke them, I have only listed those I use with my slave. You may recall that my slave uses the Nadu position when she is waiting for me in a private setting and any time we conduct our Recommitment Ritual.

Some Refinements in the Art of Service

Feeling the slave's Slavery
"After a slave is in a PRESENTING position, he or she pauses to feel the presence of their slavery. It is important for the slave to take the needed time for this — to feel the strength and dedication of their slavery, to let the rush and static of the outside world subside, and to find the peace of his slavery before addressing the Master." (Butchmann's: Feeling your slavery.)

Commentary: I consider this point to be really important. I have observed instances where a slave has appeared almost insolent in the performance of service because the slave has made only perfunctory recognition of her action. That is, the slave will serve without collecting herself and focusing on the Honor of her service. If I ask for a pen, I expect my slave to find a pen, bring it to me, kneel, focus on the pen, place it in the palms of my two hands, kiss the pen, and offer it to me. I would be disappointed in my slave's service were she simply to say: "Oh, here's a pen, Master," and pass the thing to me.

Waiting for Recognition

The slave must continue with the presenting ritual until Master recognizes her presence by a word, look, or gesture.

- If Master is busy and moving around the room when the slave enters and takes up a Standing Present position, the slave moves her eyes to follow Master's location and to not miss a hand signal or gesture to approach.

- If the slave is standing, the slave will alter her own location in the room to avoid losing track of Master. Typically, however, Master will quickly notice the slave and either allow her to complete the presenting ritual or waive that ritual by telling her to "sit," "stay," or "continue." If told to "stay," the slave remains where she is and maintains the present position until she is allowed to complete the ritual or is given another order.

Commentary: One of the most annoying problems comes from hosting a party and not being able at all times to have use of my slave. Intellectually, I understand that she is working on something relevant to a guest or to the party as a whole. But when the party is fairly small — say three other couples and there is no one to help my slave — I often find myself wishing for more backup. At any rate, when she does return, I wish her to enter and assume a standing present position until I decide where I want her to be or what I want her to do.

Presenting in Special Situations

Presenting in a Restaurant. The slave stands at the end of the booth or side of the table in the Public Present position until Master tells her to sit by word or gesture. The slave discreetly says, "Sir, yes, Sir! Thank you, Sir!" and takes her seat. If Master stands for any reason, the slave will again rise to the Public Present position — gracefully and naturally, not looking hurried, clumsy, or "put upon" — and remain in that position until Master gives a different direction.

> **Commentary:** We live this lifestyle 24/7. We are never out of protocol. It's not always High Protocol, but there is always some form of protocol being used.

An M/s Studies Book

Chapter 5

Rituals and Routines

> *The danger in ritual is that it becomes rote. You guard against this by bringing yourself present through focus and intention while completing a ritual.*

Actions Preparatory to Master's Visit

This section was prepared when **we had separate houses. I have left it in as this will apply to many situations with readers.**

State of the slave's Residence

The entire house will be tidy, with particular attention to the kitchen and bedroom. Nothing will be found on any surface other than what may be necessary for evening meal preparation. The dining room table will be set and the book the slave is reading to me will be set out.

If seasonally appropriate, the slave will set fireplace and ensure adequate firewood and kindling are available and that the fireplace is ready to be lit.

Electric lighting will be subdued throughout the house, set to a pleasing orange glow (dimmer switches set at approximately half power). Glaring lights (kitchen or hallway) will be turned off. Candles and flowers will be placed on tables as appropriate.

Drinks and appetizers will have been prepared both for Master and the slave. These will be waiting (without ice) until Master arrives. Upon hearing Master's arrival, the slave will place ice in drinks.

Appetizers — such as smoked salmon, cheeses, fruits, crackers etc. — will be prepared/arranged in an artistic manner.

> **Commentary:** While you may use any etiquette guide that suits your levels of formality, I have relied heavily on Service Etiquette, Fourth Edition by Oretha D. Swartz (Annapolis, MD: Naval Institute Press) 1988, as the basis of our family Protocols.
>
> I am highly visual and sensitive to clutter; I notice the quality of objects. Taken together, I care a great deal about the look of my slave's house and how it is maintained.

Appropriate Dress if Master is Arriving for Dinner

The slave will have showered and perfumed herself and will be Dressed. Examples of "Dressed" include:

- A man's white shirt, tie, white garter belt, white hose, heels.
- A black suit jacket, black garter belt, black hose, heels (no blouse).
- Some form of military uniform fetish wear.

At no time when the slave is Dressed may the slave wear underwear. [Note: It is my Instruction that if the slave wears underwear, it signals that she wants to be scolded and spanked.]

Appropriate Dress if Master is Arriving after Dinner

The slave may wear the white shirt outfit, a peignoir, or other informal nightwear.

State of the slave Upon Master's Arrival

Physical Position: The slave will wait in the Nadu position just inside the front door. Unless instructed otherwise, the slave will be dressed as described above. The slave will kneel-up as Master enters the door (this means rising to her knees from the Nadu position of sitting on her crossed feet).

Mental Position: The slave will be in a positive and up-beat mood, focused on being present. If there are special, troubling *issues*, slave will have communicated these to Master before Master's arrival and they will be Attended To after this ceremony ends. If there is some serious issue (death of relative; serious personal illness) that will have a negative effect upon this *greeting ritual,* and if the slave has not been able to communicate this information to Master earlier in the day, the slave **must** tell Master immediately upon his arrival.

Coming Present: At this point, we go through our *Recommitment Ceremony*, previously described.

> **Commentary:** This section described the slave's preparations for a visit FROM Master to the slave. The next section describes the slave's visit to Master OR the slave's evening preparations when staying at my home.

Preparing Master's House for an "Evening"
This section now applies, as we live together.

Everything that applied to preparing the slave's house applies equally to preparing my house. It is the slave's responsibility to carry out the final tidying and to prepare herself for the evening. In reality, I excuse the slave about 90 minutes before I wish to have cocktails and the slave begins to prepare the evening meal, the drinks and appetizers, sets the house lighting levels (previously described as this related to her house), lights the candles (after first trimming the wicks), turns on whatever music she has selected, and lights incense (if desired). The slave then showers and Dresses. Seasonally, I light the fireplace (that the slave previously prepared).

Coming Present: The next time I will see the slave, she will be appropriately Dressed. She will present herself to me and we will go through our *Recommitment Ceremony*, previously described.

> **Commentary:** This is another example of the sub-theme of this Manual/book: using the M/s dynamic as a vehicle to make every day special. We use Ceremony as the demarcation between the mundane part of life and the exceptionally special magic that we've built into our relationship.

Dining

In our Family, most evening meals are semi-formal affairs. A series of customs and rituals have evolved that make these evenings special. This section covers Family decorum during these times. Because these dinners are so stylized, I have prepared a handout that serves as a Guide to Guests. On occasion, I will email this to guests in advance of the dinner.

While most of the following comments relate to meals prepared and served at home, some references relate to behavior, actions or manners in public or at events given by others.

So, this part of the book details how to prepare the house and the meal. It explains how to set the table for the appropriate level of service and how to clear the table and clean the dishes.

Background

General Notes on Decorum: As a Family, it is our Policy to appear at home and away from home slightly *dressed up*. However, we do not seek to be conspicuous — just a little more dressed than is customary. This is also true about *behavior* and *speech*. For example, I support conventional behavior in public, better to blend with the surroundings. In terms of speech, I am sensitive to regional speech patterns my slave uses and have required that the slave eliminate them (In Texas: "I'd *like for* you to help me with this project," or "I'm *fixin' to* go to the store.") I also require my slave to correct regionally-induced grammatical errors ("There are three of them over there," as opposed to "There's three of them over there.")

> **Commentary:** One's dress, one's dialect/accent and one's articulation level telegraphs one's upbringing. If anyone wants an instant lesson in this, just watch women shopping at Sacs Fifth Avenue; listen to their speech. No, not everyone you see there will walk gracefully nor speak fluidly with high-level language skills, but the sales clerks certainly notice the difference between those whose mannerisms are polished and refined, and those that suggest less sophistication.

Rationale – Why have "Dining Protocols"? Formal dining makes a ceremony out of the *eating experience*. My idea of an Exceptional Evening includes dressing up and having a gourmet meal before hours of play. As my slave's duty is to support my vision, this section describes that vision in detail.

Dining in; Dining out

I have adapted terms used to describe formal military meal service.

> **Dining In** is the term I use to refer to *formal or semi-formal* evening meals served to Family only.

> **Dining Out** is the term I use to refer to *formal or semi-formal* evening meals that also include non-Family members.

The slave will keep a notebook of meals served for all Guests at Dining Out events. Notes will include wines served as well as the foods for each course. The slave will record all gifts brought by Guests and is responsible for preparing written thank-you notes for Master to send.

How "Formal" is this? If you read books on formal service, you will immediately realize that a true formal dinner requires a serving staff. The serving staff does *not* eat with the Host and Guests. Because I wish to eat my meals *with* my slave(s), I have modified certain aspects of the *formal dining* service to account for periods when slaves are seated at Table.

In traditional formal service, no serving platters or bowls are passed between seated guests as they would be at a "family style" meal. While my slave or her slave will take the serving dishes to each guest at the beginning of each course, occasions *do* arise when a condiment (such as gravy or cranberry sauce) will be needed again. Passing these from one person to another avoids any significant interruption in the flow of the dinner conversation. Once my slave has served the course to Master and each guest, and is then seated at the table, her remaining duty is closely to monitor water and wine levels and to take the initiative to keep them refilled.

Commentary: There are myriad ways that readers may choose to structure the meal to fit their preferred lifestyle.

Personal Table and Dinner Party Decorum and Manners
Dining Tips for High Protocol Dinners

Please turn off your cell phone before entering the house. Our evening will start with appetizers and drinks, and we will then move to the dining room for dinner. You will approach your chair from the left side (and when you get up at the end of the dinner, you will leave your chair from the right side).

Once at Table, please remain silent and respectful throughout the "Coming Present" ceremony my slave and I will share before we eat. At a formal dinner, slaves and submissives will rise as they see their Masters (or Doms) rise.

These are tips for the period before dinner is served:

- Drinks, including hard liquor beverages, may be served before dinner. Hard liquor is never consumed during the meal and any remaining beverage left in your glass when dinner is served should not be brought to Table.

- Do not attempt to converse with the service slaves while they are actively in service at the beginning of each course. This is likely to distract them from their duties.

These are tips for properly handling wine and the offering of Toasts:

- Don't touch your wine glass until Master or Mistress offers the opening Toast.

- Hold your red wine glass by the bowl, not by the stem; white wine, hold the stem, not the bowl (you don't want to warm the chilled white wine).

- When the Master or Mistress rises to give the toast, guests are also expected to rise.

- The exception is when you are being toasted individually, you remain seated and you DO NOT take a sip from the glass in your own honor.

- DO NOT offer a toast while someone else is toasting until after everyone drinks to that toast.

- It's considered good manners to ask the host for permission before proposing a toast of your own.

- Recognize your rank and be sure that when you raise your glass in toast (do not clink glasses as you could inadvertently shatter a crystal goblet).

These are tips for properly handling utensils:

- Cut only one piece of food before eating it.

- When you are not using your utensils, place them diagonally across the dinner plate's upper right edge.

- The knife blade is turned to face the center of the plate.

- When you have finished eating, place your utensils flat, diagonally across the upper 1/3 of the plate, food end pointing towards 11 and handles pointing at 3.

Managing your napkin.

- Do not touch your napkin until Mistress (or Master, in Mistress's absence) places her/his napkin in her/his lap.

- Do not fully unfold the napkin — open it to the point where it's folded in half, with the fold towards your body.

- If you have to leave Table before the meal has ended, place your napkin on your chair.

- Master will signal the end of the meal by placing his napkin on the table and indicate that it is time to clear off the table.

- At the end of the meal, place the folded napkin to the right of the dinner plate.

- Under no circumstances do you place the linen napkin on the dirty plate.

Terms and Serving Protocols Within This Family

Under normal conditions, when the two of us are dining alone, I expect my slave to don white serving gloves and begin the meal service by pouring our dinner wine. After the wine bottle has been replaced in its caddy, the slave will proceed to offer meats and vegetables from serving trays. She is expected to serve from an *honor present* position — down on one knee.

When we have company that is not part of the Leather lifestyle, or when the submissive/slave has *not* been assigned to my slave, my slave will serve the guest Dom/Domme first, then me, then the guest submissive/slave.

When we have company, and that company includes a submissive who has been placed in our service for the evening, my slave will act as First Girl and supervise any submissive in her charge. Such submissives will serve Master at his slave's direction. Whomever is serving will, upon completing that service, serve him/herself. (Note: Serving protocols when non-family members are present are covered in a later discussion of the "Order of Precedence.")

Timeliness when Invited to a Party
One of the most valuable habits that anyone can acquire is that of being on time. In our Family, we will arrive within 15 minutes of the specified starting time, particularly for a dinner party. We will not arrive before the stated start time.

Leaving a Party
Formal dinner parties often have a Guest of Honor, who will be announced when other guests are invited. In these situations, we will never leave the party before this Guest. Similarly, we will avoid staying longer than 15 minutes after the Guest of Honor has left.

If a member of our Family is the Guest of Honor, we will remain no more than 30–45 minutes after dinner is concluded. If there is no Guest of Honor, we will not remain longer than an hour after dinner is concluded.

Expressing Your Thanks
Any Family member who has been a guest at a party or Dinner is expected to write or telephone the host or hostess. That is, while a sincere expression of thanks when leaving the party is generally

sufficient, when participating in a High Leather Protocol dinner party, something more formal than a casual "thanks" is called for. After a special affair, the Host would be pleased to hear that you enjoyed his hospitality, and a note or phone call is in order.

Breakfasts and Luncheons

Breakfast – Routine
The slave will ask Master what he would like prepared for breakfast. With rare exceptions, the meal will be bacon and eggs that the slave will prepare and serve on the informal breakfast table. This meal is prepared as follows:

Freshly brewed coffee: Start brewing the coffee before anything else. Preparation: nine tablespoons of ground coffee per 12-cup coffee maker. When brewing is complete, pour into a cup, ¾ full and add powdered creamer to obtain a beige color. The coffee is poured into the cup after the bacon and eggs are served. The coffee-maker is to be turned off as soon as the coffee has completed brewing, in order not to burn the coffee.

Two strips of bacon done medium well: Place bacon on three folded sheets of paper towel, cover with one folded sheet of paper towel and microwave for three minutes or until crisp and greaseless. Place the bacon neatly (in relation to the scrambled eggs) on breakfast plate.

Two scrambled eggs, seasoned as follows: four squirts of "Liquid Smoke;" a few squirts of hot sauce of choice (I tend to prefer Louisiana Hot Sauce™); a little Lowery's Seasoned Pepper™. Cook eggs medium dry and place them attractively on the breakfast plate with parsley as decoration.

Breakfast – Holiday
Holiday breakfasts, prepared by slave(s), are served on the formal dining room table rather than on the informal kitchen table. Special Holiday table decorations will be in order: consult Master.

Flatware usually includes only knife, fork and teaspoon. If coffee is served in a mug, the teaspoon is placed to the right of the knife. If coffee is served in a coffee cup that rests in a saucer, the teaspoon is placed on the saucer.

Dishes are pre-warmed on a plate warmer. Unlike formal dinners, foods are placed on the table and passed among the diners.

Holiday Breakfast Menu 1:

- **French toast:** One egg per two pieces of bread, sugar, maple extract, cinnamon, milk.

- **Condiments:** chopped pecans; powdered sugar; real maple syrup that has been warmed in the microwave oven. [Note: Be careful when heating syrup, it will easily overheat and overflow the bottle. Remove cap from syrup container and microwave in 45-second bursts, closely monitoring syrup temperature.]

- **Two strips of bacon**, medium well done (if Others are dining with us, prepare their bacon in the manner each prefers.)

- **Whipped cream:** Place mixing bowl and blender blades AND the whipped cream in the freezer 20 min before preparing. To stabilize whipped cream, add 2 Tbsp of nonfat dry milk to every cup of whipping cream before you whip it. Add 2 Tbsp powdered sugar and 2 tsp MAPLE extract once the cream starts to set up. Whip until mixture will hold a hard peak. Place in a serving bowl with a serving spoon.

  [*A few additional Whipped cream notes*: Soupy whipped cream can be saved by adding an egg white, then chilling thoroughly and re-beating it. Adding a few drops of lemon juice to whipping cream reduces the whipping time. Whipping cream will not separate if you add ¼ tsp. unflavored gelatin per cup of whipped cream.]

- **Fresh coffee**

- **Orange juice;** Master requires ¼ tsp Sweet-N-Low™ added to his orange juice: stir.

Holiday Breakfast Menu 2:

- **Eggs,** prepared in various ways — Benedict, scrambled; fried; poached

- **Condiments** and accessories

- **Two strips of bacon**, done medium well.

- **Freshly brewed Coffee**

- **Orange juice**

Lunch vs. Luncheon

There are actually arcane rules that govern the use of the terms "lunch" "lunched" and "luncheon." Correct usage is: "Yesterday I lunched with Master Andrew;" "We should prepare lunch;" "We are having a summer luncheon."

While you can say: "Lunch is served," it is somewhat *more correct* to use "luncheon." However, to avoid sounding stiff and pretentious, "luncheon" may be reserved for special events, thus: "The holiday luncheon is served." At any rate, it's hard to think of a "luncheon" which is comprised of a peanut butter and jelly sandwich, thus:

> *A two-course summer luncheon* is comprised of fruit or seafood served with salad, followed by dessert.

> *A three-course luncheon* can include soup, main course and dessert **or** main course, salad and dessert, **or** fruit (melon or grapefruit), main course and dessert, **or** casserole, salad and dessert, **or** soufflé, salad and dessert.

A few words about soup. First, there are three general types of soups and they are served differently:

- Clear soups (or broths such as bouillon), are served in a two-handled cup, with matching plate. Clear soups are eaten with a spoon that is round with a short handle. After the bouillon or clear soup has cooled, it is appropriate to lift the cup with both hands and drink from it.

- Thicker forms of soup are placed in a shallow wide rimmed soup bowl and eaten with a spoon that is oval.

- Gumbo is eaten with a spoon that is round with a longer handle than the spoon used for a clear soup.

Second, when soup is served at a *formal* table, it is usually placed on the table after the guests are seated. When soup is served at an *informal* table, the slave may serve from a tureen placed in front of her.

Sherry often accompanies the soup course and may be the only wine served at that time. A white or red wine, or both, may be offered at formal luncheons. Iced tea is placed on a coaster on the summer table after guests are seated. The iced-tea spoon is placed to the right of the knives or above the plate at an informal meal. After the spoon is used, the bowl of the spoon is placed on the coaster. When hot tea is served, the service is the same as for coffee.

Second portions are NOT offered at a formal luncheon.

Preparations for Dining In or Dining Out

Special Preparations for Guests
Before planning the menu, the slave will contact the submissives/slaves of each guest invited to a Dining Out to ascertain any drink or dietary preferences, including food allergies. She will also verify the name preferences and name spelling for guests in order to correctly prepare name place cards.

Although the order of service has been discussed in detail for "Dining In" conditions, the service order changes once guests have been invited. This is because a senior Leatherman would outrank Mistress as Head of Family so far as the order of serving is concerned. Thus, Master will prepare an **Order of Precedence** (described later) so the slave knows how to set out the name place cards and also the order in which each person at Table is to be served.

Preparing the House
Living Room: Furniture is not out-of-place; those items that normally belong on a table or shelf are in their proper place, fireplace is set; every table lamp or oil lamp is either turned on or lit; additional candles are lit; all light-levels adjusted to an orange color cast; all flower arrangements are correct and vases are cleaned and filled with fresh water.

Kitchen: All dishes are clean and put away; counters are spotless and sanitized; floors have been swept and washed; sink is scoured; everything stored in its proper place.

Dining Room: Centerpiece is in place, place cards are in place (name spellings have been checked previously with any Guests); condiments have been placed on the table.

Throughout the house, be sure all waste paper baskets have been emptied, that there is adequate toilet paper in all bathrooms, that there is adequate facial tissue throughout the house and that all appears orderly and tidy.

Setting the Table
General Rules

- Verify that all silver is polished.

- The tablecloth and napkins should be snow white, or perhaps pastel colored, to provide a simple background on which to present the food.

- Wine glasses should be clear and uncolored in order to appreciate the color of the wine.

- Dinner plates, whether formal or everyday, white or colored, should not be highly decorated. One cannot appreciate the appearance of the food if one is distracted by complicated patterns.

- Table Decorations: According to most etiquette books, the basic formal table centerpiece is a china, silver, or porcelain bowl or tureen filled with flowers and flanked by silver candelabra or four candlesticks. For small tables, consider a single flower placed by each plate.

- In our Family, we sometimes lay a single red carnation directly on the tablecloth, parallel with the edge of the table, centered above each dinner plate. For Special Dinners, we use red roses as opposed to carnations.

- Place cards are another hallmark of the formal dinner. As previously discussed, the slave is responsible for verifying that all guest name spellings have been verified and that these cards are correctly placed in relation to the rank of each Guest — as listed on the Order of Precedence sheet (described later).

The Place Setting

Here is a diagram for a table setting for an extremely elaborate formal meal. No, my slave will not be called upon to prepare such an event, but my slave needs to have a reference resource in order to correctly select and place flatware and stemware.

Key:

a) Butter knife
b) Fish fork
c) Place fork
   (for meat or poultry course)
d) Salad or cheese fork
e) Dessert spoon and fork
f) Salad or cheese knife
g) Place knife
   (for meat or poultry course)
h) Fish knife

i) Place spoon
j) Soup spoon
k) Oyster or shellfish fork
l) Water goblet
m) Champaign glass
   (for dessert)
n) Red wine glass (for meat)
o) White wine glass (with fish)
p) Sherry glass (with soup)

Here is a photo of our daily dining room setup.

Ambiance

In general, flowers improve the look of the table. Elaborate floral arrangements are THE hallmark of a formal dinner. However, take care not to block one guest's view of another guest with the flower arrangement. If dining at a small table, a small floral arrangement or a bowl of mixed fruit may serve as the centerpiece — or place single flowers in individual vases at each place.

Candlelight adds intimacy to a dinner. The size and style of the candlesticks depend on the occasion itself, but they should never be too grandiose.

Cutlery 201

Whether silver or stainless steel, precise rules govern cutlery placement.

First, for knives and forks, there is a distinction between luncheon and dinner flatware. Dinner knives and forks are slightly larger and heavier than their luncheon counterparts.

Flatware is laid on the table according to use, starting on the outside of the place setting and working toward the plate. Forks are placed to the left of the plate, except that seafood forks are placed to the *right of the spoon, tines up*.

A fork is provided for each course unless one is expected to eat the course with a spoon. (Any time you're uncertain, copy the host or hostess.) The usual flatware placement presumes that the salad is a first course (informal dinner). So, if the meal includes salad, main, and dessert courses served in this order, the salad fork, dinner fork, and dessert fork will be placed in the same order to the left side of the dinner plate. When salad is served following the main course (formal dinner), the salad fork is placed next to the plate.

The various knives are placed immediately to the right of the plate, also in the order of the dish being served, from the outside toward the inside. Salad and dessert knives are provided if they're likely to be needed for cutting tomatoes or wedges of lettuce in the salad course or fruit in the dessert course. The spoons are placed to the right of all the knives, again in the order of the courses for which they're needed, again from the outside toward the inside.

Teaspoons or place spoons (larger) on the informal luncheon or dinner table are used for soup served in cups or for fruit. Teaspoons on the breakfast table are for grapefruit, cereals and the like. Before serving tea or coffee, teaspoons are placed on the saucers at the right of the handles. At **formal dinners**, dessert spoons and/or forks are brought in on the dessert plate. Fork on the left, spoon on the right. At **informal meals,** the dessert spoon and/or fork may be placed on the table, centered above the dinner plate.

An exception is made for utensils such as the iced tea spoon, because it might be needed throughout the meal, and thus remains to the left of all other spoons. Utensils specific to each course are removed at the end of the course.

Tableware 201
If you like to provide a bread plate (required at a formal dinner), this should be placed to the left of the fork with the individual butter spreader

placed across the top edge of the bread plate. If you are serving antipasto (an appetizer usually consisting of an assortment of foods such as smoked meats, cheese, fish, and vegetables), provide a side plate on top of the dinner plate. If beginning with pasta, place a smaller dish on top of the dinner plate; this will serve as the pasta plate.

At the end of a course, plates are removed from the left and clean plates are placed from the right.

Stemware 201
More good wine has been ruined by a malodorous glass than anything else. Always **smell** a glass before pouring wine in it. Wine glasses have two common causes of bad smells: insufficient rinsing that leaves a detergent or chlorine smell, or absorption of environmental odors such as the scent of wood from the cupboard, cardboard from a storage box, or cooking odors. Re-wash or at least rinse it out if you smell anything.

Stemware is placed above and to the right side of the plate. If more than one drink is served to each person, position each piece of glassware along a line slanting slightly towards the dinner knife. The dessert and the glass for the wine accompanying the dessert may also be brought to the table together. Stemware is arranged in order of use, starting from the right. Thus, the first glass is always the water glass, then the various wine glasses arranged according to the order that they will be used with the various courses.

Please see Appendix C for a resource concerning wine selection as a function of the food being served. From there, you can derive the type of wine glasses that will be set out.

For example, the order that follows presumes that a fruit or fish dish will be followed by a meat dish and that a dessert will be served.
- Water
- White wine
- Red wine
- Dessert wine

Table Service – Details

Table Linen: The traditional formal dinner table is covered with a white or ivory-colored damask tablecloth. A silence pad should be placed over the table and under the tablecloth. A lace or linen tablecloth for formal dining affairs must not overhang the edge of the table. Linen placemats may be used on top of the tablecloth.

Napkins: Napkins should match the table linen service. In formal dining, white and off-white napkins are used; one doesn't wish to detract from the place settings. If the china is solid white, take care that the napkin color is complimentary. Napkin size varies with the function:

- 24" square — very formal dinner

- 18–22" square — less formal multi-course meal

- 12" x 20" (called "lapkins") are for a buffet service where a one-dish menu is eaten from the lap

- 14–16" square — luncheon service

- 12" square (held under a tea plate) — used for afternoon tea

- Cocktail napkins — when folded properly in quarters, are about 1/3rd the size of the luncheon napkin

Table China: It is customary for all plates used at one time to match. That is, one may change out the pattern of plates between the main course and the dessert course if the plates don't come from the same pattern.

Chargers: Chargers are decorative elements that are placed underneath plates to add color or texture to the table. Each plate should be set in the center of the place setting and place settings should be set equidistant from each other. The rest of the components used to set a formal table will be set with the dinner plate in mind. The charger will generally be removed just before the main course. Note: If a charger is used, soup and melon bowls will be placed on top of it. Then the entire setting (charger and soup or melon bowls) will be removed before the next course is presented.

Water Pitcher: Water is frequently overlooked by those unused to providing more formal dinners. The water pitcher — made of cut glass

— is an item for the table that contributes to the air of formality. Be sure that all water glasses — and the water pitcher — are filled just before everyone is seated. The pitcher of water should remain on the table throughout the meal.

Serving Dishes: The sizes of serving dishes and platters vary as a function of the number of guests you intend to serve routinely. You will generally need serving dishes appropriate to serve the following.

- Vegetable dishes
- Soft dishes such as fruit compote (bowl required)
- Fruits and desserts (shallow bowl required)
- Bread tray or basket
- Sauceboat or gravy boat
- Small oval platter for meats or fish
- Large oval platter for large roasts (or cold meats at a buffet)
- Round platter or cake stand (a cake plate on a pedestal) for serving pies, cakes, cookies etc.

Salt and Pepper: It is a hallmark of a formal dinner that each guest have individual salt and pepper shakers at their place setting.

Wine caddy: Wine bottles are placed in a wine caddy, not directly on the tablecloth. This is done to avoid having an errant drip of wine fall onto the fine table linen. If serving chilled wines, a wine bucket is set on the sideboard table. The wine bucket must be placed on a plate in order to protect the wooden sideboard from getting wet from the condensate that will drip from the sides of the iced bucket.

Pre-seating Preparation:
Our pre-seating checklist follows:

Table-Check Checklist	Yes
Candles are of sufficient length to last throughout the dinner – change if necessary.	
Everything silver upon the table is adequately polished and polish if necessary.	
Silver wine caddy is on the table and that the evening's bottle of dinner wine is placed upon it.	
Verify that the dinner setting (both the plate and silverware) are ONE INCH from table's edge.	
If the forks are placed on a napkin, that napkin must be one inch from table's edge.	
Verify that place cards have been correctly placed in relation to the rank of each Guest and that all guest name spellings have been checked.	
Verify that there is no errant candle wax that has dripped onto the candle holder.	

Checklist of Items Placed on or Near the table	Yes
Apple sauce or mint jelly or cranberry sauce	
Salt/pepper	
Filled water glasses	
Open bottle of wine	
Place a full water pitcher on the sideboard	
If salad dressing is to be applied by diners AT the table, then this dressing must be placed on the table before diners are seated.	

Special Conditions	Yes
Be sure to open all red dinner wines at least 30 minutes before dinner is to be served.	
If any diners prefer grape juice to wine, their glasses must be filled before the Call to Dinner.	
If salad is to be served, salad plates will be placed in the freezer when dinner preparation begins and removed shortly before dinner so that the plate is chilled before serving the salad.	
For an informal meal, include the coffee cup and saucer with the table setting. Otherwise, bring them to the table with the dessert.	

Menus

(As a footnote to history, in the Military Services, the traditional *formal meal* includes standing prime rib roast and Yorkshire pudding.)

Four courses:
- Seafood cocktail (white wine)
- Soup
- Entrée (red wine)
- Cheese and fruit (dessert wine)

Five courses:
- Seafood cocktail (white wine)
- Soup
- Entrée (red wine for meat, white wine for fish)
- Salad
- Cheese and fruit (dessert wine)

Sequence of Courses	Wine
Shrimp Cocktail	White Burgundy*
Soup - usually clear	Sherry
Fish, hot or cold	White Rhine*
Main course of meat and vegetables	Merlot or Claret
Main course of game and vegetables	Burgundy
Salad	No new wine
Dessert (ice cream, sherbet, ect)	Champagne
Fresh Fruit (pears, grapes, ect)	Champagne
* serve chilled	

Matching wine to the food course (see also Appendix C)

Wine Serving Temperatures

Wine service is as much art as science. Professional advice instructs that wines should be offered at the following temperatures, depending upon the kind of wine:

- "Young" whites   50–53 degrees
- "Mature" whites   53–57 degrees
- Rosé   53–57 degrees
- "New" reds   50–57 degrees
- "Mature" reds   61–65 degrees
- Sparkling wines   50–53 degrees
- Sweet wines   50–65 degrees

Rolls, Coffee, Mints

- While bread is optional, rolls are always served at formal dinners. However, using bread plates for rolls is optional and depends upon space at Table.
- Coffee is always served at formal dinners.
- Mints are frequently served after the final course.

Cocktail and Appetizer Service Protocols

Serving Cocktails

The slave will be gloved when serving drinks. Drinks will be placed on a serving tray when brought into a room. Drinks will be arranged on the tray such that Master's drink is placed forward of all other drinks. Before drinks are offered to any Guest, the slave will offer a drink to Master from a *Full Present* position. Drinks are then offered to Guests from the tray according to the Order of Precedence previously prepared for the slave's use (and described later in this book).

Serving Wine

Mentioned previously, it is important to give the wine bottle a rotating twist at the very end of the pouring cycle to ensure a dripless result. My slave will pour a small amount of wine into my glass. Master will sample the wine and signal whether to continue filling his glass or reject the bottle and open another. Once Master's glass has been filled, the slave will continue filling glasses according to the Order of Precedence.

Serving Appetizers

Servers will be gloved when serving appetizers. If Mistress is present, Master will serve her. If Mistress is NOT present, my slave will serve Master first from a Full Present position, then serve Guests. If the slave has her own submissive present, she will only serve Master, then signal her submissive to serve Guests.

Dressing for the Evening

Levels of Dress

Family events call for one of six levels of dress.

1) **Family dress**: Casual: think "shopping at the mall." Black jeans are preferred but khakis (for men) are acceptable. Clothing should be starched and pressed.

2) **Silks**: May be worn before 6 PM. For men: black dress slacks (wool preferred) and long-sleeved silk shirt or dress shirt with open neck. An ascot would be appropriate. Jacket optional. For women: anything classy that would be appropriate in public.

3) **Fetish dress**: Any fetish clothing that is less formal than military Mess Dress. Women wear garter belt, hose and heels. My slave sometimes wears a man's white dress shirt, tie optional, with white garter belt, white hose and gold sequined heels.

4) **Mess Dress**: May not be worn before 6 PM; men will wear a short-waisted mess dress service jacket: Mess Dress, when worn with a standard pleated semi-formal shirt with collar, gold links, studs and black bow tie is called Mess Dress Blue by the military. As this applies to the Family, Master

wears the Mess Dress jacket, but is generally shirtless. My slave wears a black Mess Dress uniform with black garter belt and hose with black stiletto heels.

5) **Evening dress** – Black tie – or Evening Mess Dress (worn with a stiff bodice wing collar formal shirt, white bow tie, white vest, and pearl links and studs). May not be worn before 6 PM. Black tuxedo jacket or white tuxedo jacket are appropriate. For women, black suit jacket, black garter belt, black hose, black stiletto heels. Long black skirt is optional.

6) **Full formal** – White tie and tails. Boutonnieres other than white or red carnations may be worn in the left buttonhole. After 6 PM except during the summer: Tails for men and floor-length black gown for women.

7) **Family Ceremony** – Cutaway jackets (gray) are seldom worn by the Family, and are reserved for very special Family ceremonies.

Boutonnieres

Boutonnieres are NOT routinely used within our Family. (As an aside, do NOT wear a boutonniere when wearing military decorations.)

Dress Handkerchief

Family Protocols call for a red or black silk handkerchief used with tuxedo and tails — this is an optional item. However, our formal dress protocols in a vanilla setting call for a dress handkerchief that is white (this handkerchief may be initialed with a single letter or with all of one's initials. For evening use, the initials are white, gray or black.) Other handkerchief colors may be worn during the day and, if chosen, should blend with one's tie.

Gloves

During serving rituals: The slave(s) will wear white cotton service gloves during all serving rituals — drinks or food. In order to begin serving, the slave will don white gloves immediately after our *Coming Present* ceremony when Mess Dress, Evening Dress or Full Formal Dress is worn.

Medals and Awards

Considering that we have not had the honor of serving in the military, we are cautious about the use of service medals for fetish dress. I tend to wear a gold-colored hand-cuff tie-tack on my mess dress lapels.

If you have earned service medals or awards, the protocol I recommend is: miniature medals are worn with Mess Dress, Semiformal Dress and Dress Whites. Ribbons are worn with Mess Dress, Evening Dress and Full Formal.

Dining Protocols

Rules Governed by the Level of Service

Formal Plated Service means that the slave will serve from left and remove from left. The slave will serve one plate at a time using her left hand. If the slave must serve a condiment, she will carry only one condiment at a time. This is gloved service.

Informal Plated Service means that the slave will serve from left, remove from right. In this case, the slave will approach the table carrying two full dinner plates, walk between two seated guests and first serve the guest to her right with the plate in her right hand, then serve the guest to her left with the plate in her left hand. Once everyone has been served their main course, the slave will then return to the table bearing trays of condiments, one in each hand. In this case, she will offer these condiments to guests one at a time, offering first the bowl in her right hand, then the bowl in her left hand. This is ungloved service.

Rules Governing Table Service

Essentials of Service Service at Formal Table must be efficient, quiet and unobtrusive. Nothing is ever taken directly from a slave's hands.

- If a guest is being brought something that the guest will take from the slave and place on the table, then the slave will bring that item to table on a serving tray. That tray is held with right hand centered underneath the tray (right = submissive side) with the slave's left hand at her side [Note: This is the opposite of traditional formal service, where the tray is carried in the *left* hand. Never one to be troubled by inconsistency, we'll switch back to the traditional service mode in a few paragraphs.]

- If a guest is being brought something that will be transferred from a bowl onto the guest's plate, the slave may hold that bowl in her gloved hands while the guest serves him or herself.

Rules of Service – initial course, plated service – formal meal. When the slave places the initial plate in front of the Guest, it is presented from the guest's left side using the slave's *left* hand (because of the angle of service). The plate rests in the palm of the slave's gloved hand and she uses her right hand to effect the plate's transfer from her left palm to the place setting. [Note: In traditional formal service, the dish or platter rests on a folded napkin placed on the flat of the servant's ungloved hand. We do NOT follow that protocol.]

Changing courses – plated service, formal meal. To ensure gracefulness, our protocol for changing plates during a course change involves two steps rather than the traditional one step. First, the slave removes the used plate from the table, placing it on the empty portion of the tray held by her assistant. Next, she removes a fresh plate from the same tray and, placing it in the palm of her left hand, now places it before the guest.

Note #1: If my slave is serving alone, then we're back to the traditional single one-step process: she carries the fresh dish in *right* hand and after using her *left* hand to remove the used dish, places the fresh dish before the guest.

Note #2: We've had to revert to the traditional use of the right hand to carry the new dish because right-handed people would find it easier to stabilize a full plate using their strongest hand.

Changing Courses – plated service, informal meal. Two dishes are removed at one time and two fresh dishes are brought to Table at one time.

Changing Courses – two servers. My slave's assistant will stand with a large tray containing the plated next course and sufficient room to place a used dish; my slave (formally called the Table Server) will place a used dish on tray and then remove a fresh dish from the tray and place it in front of the Guest.

The table linen is cleared of crumbs before dessert. A "crumber" will be used for this task. The slave will hold the crumb tray below the table level to the left of the Guest and use the crumber brush to sweep the table surface to remove the offending object. Place cards are also removed at this time.

Dinner Seating Protocols

Starting Time. The starting time for dinners will usually be 8 PM, but this is at Master's sole discretion. When Harvey starts to play the piano, everyone knows that it's time to move from the living room to Table. (Remember the Jimmy Stewart movie about the invisible rabbit? I have a computer-driven player piano that I refer to as "Harvey." So, "Harvey" plays for us throughout dinner.)

So, once Harvey starts to play, Master will signal and then escort the appropriate person to the dining room. "Appropriate person" is determined thus: Mistress (if present) or my slave, if this is a *Dining In* and Mistress is NOT present. If this is a *Dining Out*, then the most senior guest will be the *appropriate person* to be escorted to Table.

How to Take your Chair Once it's Your Turn to Do So. All dinner guests will be seated from the left side of the chair and will rise from their seats from the right side of the chair.

Who Sits First? Master will seat Mistress first, as Head of Family. Master will then seat any Guest Femme Domme. Master will then signal other Doms/Masters to be seated but he will remain standing. When it comes to submissives, guest submissives will be seated after all their Doms/Masters have been seated. Family submissives will be seated in order of their rank/seniority, the most junior being the last to sit.

What Happens Next? Once everyone has been seated, Master will conduct his *"Centering Ritual."* This takes place before napkins are placed in the lap.

Centering Ritual: This ritual occurs before Master takes his seat. It is conducted so that the recipient can feel the special moment of this repast. It is a time of special bonding between Master and his submissives. It is important that all Family and Guests are utterly silent during this phase of the dinner rituals. Master will engage in his "Centering Ritual" with all Family submissives who are *at table* in order of their seniority.

[Note: I'm not going to describe this ritual. You are invited to make up your own or ask me via email.]

When the ritual is over, Master will take his seat and then remove his napkin from the table and place it in his own lap. This is the signal that everyone else may then remove their own napkins from table and place them in their laps. **This is also the signal for the slaves who are serving to rise and begin that process.**

Dinner Napkin Protocols

Napkin Handling: At the beginning of a meal, everyone puts their napkin in their laps, folded in half — not fully opened. The fold of the napkin is closest to your body, not your knees. During the meal, if you have to leave the table, place your napkin in your chair. At the end of a meal place your napkin to the right of your dinner plate. *Be careful not to place your napkin ON your used dinner plate.*

How to Know the Meal has Ended: The signal that the meal has ended occurs by Master placing his napkin on the table.

Dinner Service Protocols

Order of Precedence: In designing the Order of Precedence chart, there are at least two possibilities:

1) To seat the next highest ranking person to the right of the highest ranking person, and the third highest ranking person right of the second highest, etc., and continue until the person of lowest rank sits left of the highest ranking person, or

2) To begin with the second highest ranking person to the right of the highest ranking person, then put the third highest ranking person to the left of the highest ranking person, and continue alternating to the left and right until the lowest ranking person is positioned furthest from the highest ranking.

Master will determine the seating pattern and provide the slave with the typed list.

Serving and Removing Plates: As previously noted, if this is an *informal* diner, the slave will serve from left, remove from right. If this is a *formal* dinner, then the slave will serve from left and remove from left. In either case, drinks — water and wine — are served and refilled from the RIGHT.

When a plated dish is placed before a diner, the slave will rotate the plate in such a way to ensure that the meat course is at 6 o'clock (closest to the seated diner).

Refilling a Glass with Water or Wine: If the slave is refilling a **water glass**, she will pick up the glass and add the water/ice while the glass is positioned over the carpet to the right and slightly behind the Guest. If the slave is refilling a **wine glass** pour the wine into the glass where it sits on the table — do NOT pick up the wine glass. If a left-handed person moves their glass (or glasses) to the left side of the table setting, the slave may pour from their left side to avoid reaching across them. Some people may hold the glass up to pour: watch out for this because an accident may occur.

Serving Protocols:
Pouring Wine: My slave always pours the wine, whether or not a supporting slave is present. This is solely her honor. She will wear gloves and have a white linen kitchen cloth over her left forearm with which to address any accidental spills. As previously mentioned, when wine is poured it is important to give the bottle a rotating twist at the very end of the pouring cycle to ensure that no dripping occurs. The slave will pour a small amount of wine into Master's glass. As previously mentioned, Master will sample the wine and signal whether to continue filling his glass or reject the bottle and open another. Once Master's glass has been filled, the slave will continue filling glasses according to the Order of Precedence, filling her own glass last. The slave will then take her seat while her own submissive begins the food service. If sherry glasses are used during the first course, they are removed by the slave's submissive, or by the slave if there

is no slave's submissive, after the salad course. Other wine glasses remain on the table throughout the meal.

Serving Food – Non-Plated Meal: The slave will be gloved. My slave will serve Master *first* from a kneeling position, then serve Guests by remaining standing and by lowering the served item within range of the guest's plate. The slave will position serving utensils within easy reach of the person being served. If my slave has her own submissive present, my slave will serve only Master, then re-take her seat and signal her submissive to serve the remaining Family members and/or Guests in order of precedence.

Beginning the Dinner
Summary of the Process of Starting Dinner:

- Everyone moves from the living room to the dining room upon the signal from Master.

- Master seats his slave. Other Doms take their seats. Remaining submissives take their seats.

- Everyone remains silent as Master performs *Centering Ritual* with his slave.

- My slave rises and begins to serve food. At a formal meal, the slave's submissive will now be given the signal from my slave to rise from his/her seat and begin food service.

- After the food is served, Master first offers a series of structured Toasts (you will have to design your own). Once these Toasts are completed, Master may offer another toast or ask an Honored Guest to offer a toast. Note: The toast may be a seated or standing toast depending upon the formality of the event.

- Master removes his napkin from its place on the table and puts it in his lap; everyone else takes this as their signal to remove their napkins from the table and put it in their laps.

How to Hold Wine and Liquor Glasses: The thumb and first two fingers at the base of the bowl hold long-stemmed water and red wine glasses. Chilled wine is held by the stem in such a way as not to warm the glass and, by extension, the wine. Tumblers are held near the base. Brandy snifters are cupped in the palm of the hand in order to warm the brandy.

Toasts: It is disrespectful for anyone NOT to participate in a toast. All who have notified my slave that they are non-drinkers will find their wine glasses have been filled with grape juice, or other suitable juice or flavored water for this ritual. When giving a Toast at a *formal* meal, everyone will STAND *unless* you are the person *receiving the toast* — in which case, you remain seated while everyone else stands. If this is an *informal* meal, everyone remains seated while the toast is offered.

- **Timing of the Toasts**: Once all food has been served, the most senior Head of Family who accepts that responsibility will offer a Toast.

- **Offering the Toast**: The person offering the Toast will raise his/her glass and offer the Toast. Once the Toast has been offered, everyone present will raise (but not touch) glasses.

"Beginning to Eat" **Protocols with slaves and submissives**: After food has been plated but before any Family submissives may eat, Master takes a bite of food. At that signal, everyone at table — except the Family slaves/submissives — may begin to eat.

Next, Master will feed each Family slave and submissive a small forkful of food from his plate. If my slave has a submissive helping her, she will signal him/her when to eat. Once all the Family submissives have been provided a morsel, they may begin eating.

How to use your flatware — American Style – cutting food:

- **Fork** is held in the left hand, tines down, index finger on back of fork's stem pinning the food (such as a piece of meat).

- **Knife** is held in the right hand, index finger on back of knife blade. Cut one single piece of meat, use the knife if necessary to unpin the food from the fork, and then put the knife down onto the plate — blade facing toward the center of the plate. Unless you eat in the left-handed "European Style," transfer the fork to right hand — tines up — push the fork tines underneath, not into, the piece of food to pick it up. You may use your knife as a "pusher" if you need help getting foodstuffs onto your fork. Put the food in your mouth and replace the fork on plate, tines up, below your knife, which should be resting diagonally across the upper right rim of the plate.

- **Spoons**: The *dessertspoon* is longer than the *teaspoon* and is placed on the dessert plate at formal or informal meals. The *teaspoon* should appear in the saucer of the coffee cup, when served. The *soupspoon* is longer than the dessertspoon OR the teaspoon and has an oval bowl. It is only used with crème soups. Remember to use a soupspoon by dipping it towards the back of the bowl, starting with the side of the spoon that's *away* from yourself, and pushing it towards the back of the bowl. This technique will help you keep your soup off of your clothes, because any drip will be more likely to travel forward underneath the spoon and land in your mouth than to fall directly off the bottom of the spoon. Try to avoid scraping the bottom of the soup bowl. When you are done with the spoon, place it on the soup plate to the right-hand side of the bowl.

Table Manners – General

Your mother was right: table manners DO count. Here is my version of a "critical list." My slave is expected to follow these at all times.

- Do not bring your cocktail glass to Table.

- Diners should have the same number of courses and start and finish at approximately the same time. That is, diners should monitor eating progress of their peers and speed up or slow down, as necessary. If my slave and I are dining alone, she is not to finish before me.

- Once you pick up a piece of cutlery, you should never put it back on the table. (Exception: If a "knife rest" has been provided, you may place your knife there between courses.)

- It is very impolite to season your food before you have tasted it. It is an insult to the Chef who prepared the meal and thereby, it is also an insult to your host.

- Cut only enough food for the next mouthful.

- Do not speak with food in your mouth. Chew with your mouth closed and don't smack or crunch.

- Do not blow on hot liquids to cool them; stir them with a spoon and then test the temperature by taking a small spoonful of the liquid.

- Each Guest must take (and eat) a small portion from every serving dish. Nothing may be passed by.

- Do not "load up" your fork with food; dainty is good.

- If something is slightly out of reach at Table, ask that it be passed to you; do NOT start to rise out of your seat to reach for it, and do not reach in front of anyone else at the table to get something that you could have reached. Take the passed dish (or bread basket) from the person and thank them in a clear and deliberate voice. *Do not select an item from the dish (or basket) while the other guest is holding it.*

- Never lick your fingers after they have contacted food; your napkin is for that purpose.

- If you MUST remove something from your mouth (olive pit, piece of gristle) cover your mouth with your napkin, cup your other hand in front of your mouth to receive the rejected item. Place it as unobtrusively as you can upon your dinner plate.

- Never rub your lips with a napkin, pat them. Pat your mouth with your napkin before drinking from your wine or water glass to avoid leaving oils, grease or food particles on the rim of the glass.

- Soupspoons: For clear soups only, do NOT place the entire spoon inside your mouth; sip the soup from the side of the spoon. Do not slurp the liquid. (For cream soups, you may place the entire spoon in your mouth.)

- Leave the soupspoon IN the soup bowl but do not leave the soupspoon in a bouillon cup or a cream soup bowl.

- Break bread and rolls in half with your fingers, then into single-bite pieces that you place in your mouth. Do NOT cut breads with a knife. Do NOT take a bite from the broken piece of bread or roll and place the remainder back onto the bread plate.

- If butter and/or jam is served, after transferring a small portion from the serving dish to your bread plate, spread the butter on individual bites of bread, not on the entire side of the bread or roll.

- Jams and condiments go onto the bread plate first, not directly onto the bread.

- Keep arms and elbows OFF the table in the U.S. (until you have completed each course, at which point it is generally considered acceptable to lean on the table in order to hear conversations better). On the European Continent, it is customary to rest your forearm ON the table so that your hands are in clear view. The exception in the U.S. is that between courses you may momentarily rest your forearms on the table so long as you do not turn your back on your partner.

- Don't slump at the table. Sit forward in your chair, showing your interest in the conversation.

- Avoid curling your feet around the chair legs; similarly, avoid stretching your feet out under the table.

- When you finish your meal, DON'T push your plate back. Leave it alone.

- The slave(s) will remove any crumbs that have fallen onto the table. Don't touch anything that has fallen onto the table surface.

- Place your napkin in your chair when leaving the Table temporarily, otherwise place the napkin to the right of the place setting at the end of the meal when leaving the table; NEVER place your napkin on a used plate.

Table Manners – Restaurant Dining

My slave will follow these additional Rules when dining outside the home. While these Rules are written as though I am serving as Host, they apply equally if another person is hosting the meal.

- The slave will not speak directly to the waitstaff, but convey any preferences to Master, who will then order for the slave and convey preferences to the waitstaff.

- Without asking specific permission, the slave will not order a main course that takes longer to prepare than the main course that I order.

- Do not request that I order a meal for you that is more expensive than the meal that I order *unless* I specifically recommend a meal to you that is pricey.

- Order food that is easy to eat, not too messy. This is particularly relevant if we are entertaining Others at a restaurant. For example, it's often difficult to look bright and witty if you're fighting with your angel-hair pasta.

- As previously mentioned, taste first, season second. In this setting, Others will notice if you season your food without first tasting it. In the world of business, this suggests that you reach conclusions without assessing the facts.

- If you do not like the food or the way it was prepared, keep this information to yourself unless a food-safety issue is involved. I *do not* like food discussed at the table. We are dining out to have a good time, not to discuss the meal.

- Foods you can touch with your fingers include:
  - artichoke
  - asparagus (may be eaten with the fingers as long as it is not covered with sauce or otherwise prepared so it is too mushy to pick up easily)
  - bread
  - chips, French fries, fried chicken and hamburgers
  - corn on the cob
  - cookies
  - crisp bacon (but not limp bacon)
  - hors d'oeuvres, canapes, crudités (anything served at a cocktail party)
  - olives, celery and pickles
  - sandwiches that are not open-faced, not too tall to fit in the mouth, not saturated with dripping sauces or loaded

with mushy fillings; that is, sandwiches that are intended to be picked up and eaten — otherwise use your fork and knife

- o small fruits and berries on the stem, most often, fresh strawberries with the hulls attached

Monitoring Guests During the Meal

The slave will closely monitor water and wine glasses and guests' plates. From time to time, the slave will arise from Table and re-fill water and wine glasses for all guests and for Master. If a guest appears to be a hearty diner and has completed his or her serving, the slave will arise and offer a second helping for that Guest or for Master.

Changing Courses Protocols

When multiple courses are involved, the slave(s) will do two things: use a crumber to remove any food or crumbs that have fallen onto the table surface; clear away the plate belonging to the prior course and bring the prepared plate for the ensuing course. [Note: Protocols for changing plates for a multi-course meal have already been presented.]

Dinner Ending Protocols

Finishing a Meal: The slave will take extreme care *never* to end her meal before Master.

Getting the Signal: Master will signal the end of dinner and escort the appropriate person to the living room. "Appropriate person" is determined thus: Mistress (if present) or my slave, if this is a *Dining In*, and Mistress is NOT present. If this is a *Dining Out*, then the most senior person at Table will be given the signal to rise and begin the trip to the living room.

Getting Up from Table: At a formal dinner, slaves and submissives will rise as they see their Masters (or Doms) rise.

Proceeding to Living Room: Guests will be escorted to the living room. The slave will ask each Guest for his/her preference of liqueurs and selections will be brought out on serving tray. After liqueurs have been served, slave(s) will proceed to clear Table.

Table Clearing Protocol: The slave is not to stack the china plates when removing them from the table. Carry one plate per hand per trip. Remove dishes to the kitchen and soak them in the rubber tub that fits inside the sink. Take care to be as quiet as possible.

Cleanup Immediately After Company Leaves

Dining Room
Entirely clear the table. Remove all the table linen and place it in the laundry room to be dealt with later. Clean and then remove/store the table's silence pad (if used).

Clean the table. If it is a wooden table, clean with Pledge®; if it is a glass table, clean with Windex®.

Reset the table with a formal setting for three people. To summarize: in one stack, stack the plates as follows: Charger plate; dinner plate; salad plate. Flatware as follows: Knife and teaspoon to the right of the stack of plates, salad and dinner forks to the left of the stack of plates. Our Family protocol calls for a diagonal placement of the water and wine glasses as described above. The name card holders are centered two inches above the top of the plates. In our Family, the cards for Master, Mistress and my slave are always set. Master is positioned to the right of Mistress, my slave to my right (thus, I'm in the middle). Replace the candles and flowers. Be sure there is no wax upon the candleholder. If candleholder is silver, verify that it is polished. Replace the salt and pepper shakers and the wine caddy.

Kitchen
Dishes: Hand wash everything; do not use dishwasher — too harsh on the china and silver. Use the dishwasher as a drying rack for plates. Use Dawn® kitchen soap. Use rubber gloves.

Stemware: Hand wash using lukewarm water; rinse well under running water. To obtain extra sparkle, hold the glasses over some steaming water for 30 seconds. Use a lint-free linen towel without any fabric softener to dry stem and glassware. Hold the glass by the bowl, not the stem, which is fragile, and gently polish off the water. Don't force the towel into the bowl as the glass is thin and might break. Just leave the glass turned upside down and let it drain itself onto a towel before final touching-up with the linen towel.

Scour the kitchen sink and related counters. Use Cameo® to scour a stainless steel kitchen sink; use Barkeeper's Friend® for a porcelain sink. Also use Barkeeper's Friend® to clean all kitchen counter surfaces. Use 409® to clean the stovetop and stove vent. Use a paper towel to dry the sink and counters after cleaning.

An M/s Studies Book

Chapter 6

Note about Chapter 6: This material is personal to our family and therefore I have written it to my slave — not to an unknown reader.

The slave's Job as Personal Assistant

"It's My personal belief that once My slave enters into service to Me, everything it does is some form of service to Me. Breathing is a form of service. Striving to spread a smile at work is a form of service. Maintaining the slave quarters is a form of service. All the chopping-wood/carrying-water of life is a form of service. The idea here is to encourage My slave to view EVERYTHING as an opportunity to be of service to Me; thereby manifesting deeper connection to all of humanity/the universe."

Officer Wes, Private letter 2006

Maid Services

House Care – Cleanup, Day after Entertaining

Process the linen napkins; wash them by hand. Either iron the napkins after they have dried or dry them by wringing them out and stretching them flat on the clean kitchen counter, taking care to remove all air bubbles (this is a natural way of creating a napkin that will look as though it has been ironed).

Fold the napkins per House Protocol and place the necessary number on the top service plate. Extra napkins go in the linen closet.

Vacuum all living room and dining room carpets. Use Endust® when dusting. Use Liquid Gold® or Pledge® on kitchen chairs and on all wood furniture. Verify that all surfaces are neat and tidy; all books and magazines put away; play toys sanitized and replaced.

Mop all tile floors. Use Mr. Clean® (orange scented) detergent. "Load" the mop in this solution. Mop a section of floor, rinse the mop under tap water, NOT back in the detergent solution, then re-load the mop in detergent solution and continue mopping.

Fully clean all bathrooms. Clean commode and sink and mop the floors. Fold the last sheet of toilet paper to a point to signal that the room has been cleaned. If necessary, wash the throw rug(s). Clean all counters, leaving *nothing* on them. Clean all mirrors with Windex®.

House Care – General Standing Orders
Level One Cleaning
Vacuum heavily used areas, particularly in the Master bath and closet and in the Master bedroom.

Ensure all surfaces are neat and tidy, nothing out of place. In the Master bath, be sure that the towels are cleaned, if necessary, and that they are hung up correctly. Polish the chrome water faucets on the vanity, in the bath and in the shower. Be sure that the counter surfaces are "sponged."

In the Master bedroom, make the bed and change sheets if needed. Be sure that all surfaces are dusted if needed. Be sure that nothing that can be put away is left out.

In the kitchen, spray all stovetop and counter surfaces with 409® and wipe them clean. Put away all dishes. Polish the chrome faucets and either wipe out or scour the sink, depending upon its condition.

Our Family Protocol calls for both the dining room and informal kitchen tables to be set — do that after the kitchen is cleaned.

Attend to the playroom or other rooms in the house, as needed (little, if anything, should be needed).

Do load(s) of laundry and iron, as needed. Empty all the house trashcans.

Level Two Cleaning. As above, plus...
Use cleanser (Bartenders Friend®, not Ajax®) on all Formica surfaces. Use cleansers on all sinks in all bathrooms and the kitchen. Clean the tile around the shower door. Use 409® on stove vent area and on stove back-splashes. Vacuum the remainder of the house.

Clean ashes out of fireplace; sweep hearth. Seasonally, ensure adequate firewood is on clean hearth. Sweep and mop kitchen floor; check all woodwork around light switches and door handles for smudge marks; remove same.

Run an empty load through the dishwasher and ensure that it is spotless, inside and out.

Clean all windowsills.

Level Three Cleaning: As above, plus...
Dust the house, including picture frames, wooden bowls and furniture surfaces. Scour the shower/bathtub(s).

Vacuum all floors that need also to be mopped. Mop all floors, including bathroom floors. Wash all bathroom rugs and clean all mirror surfaces.

Remove everything from refrigerator and clean all surfaces. Clean top of refrigerator, washer and dryer; clean inside microwave and inside oven.

Lift out and clean all stove burners; lift the entire stove surface and clean below the elements. Replace any aluminum "protectors" that fit immediately below the heating elements.

Check AC filters — and change if necessary.

Level Four Cleaning: As above, plus
Clean all baseboards and woodwork; clean all windows, inside only. Clean all ceiling fan blades. Clean the freezer.

Valet Services

Preparing New Boots
The slave will follow these Protocols for *new boots* that aren't oil tanned. The purpose is to get the new boots to shine and to keep them shining with ease.

Beware: New boots are not easy to work with. Most new boots have a coating on them that will keep them looking new for many years. This coating must come off in order to get the polish to stick. Not all boots are equal. The more they cost, the more coating they will have on them.

Supplies:
- Rubbing alcohol
- Scrub sponges
- Soft cloth — preferably cheesecloth

Actions to take:

1) In a small bowl, soak a sponge in a solution of equal parts of water and alcohol.

2) Use the sponge to rub the boot lightly in small circles to take off the coating mentioned above. (WARNING: This can be tricky. The slave must be very careful not to scratch the leather. Scratched leather will require additional work.)

   The slave will notice that as she repeatedly dips the sponge in the water/alcohol mix, it starts looking milky. That means that the slave is successfully removing the undesired coating. If the mix becomes too milky, change it for a fresh mix. Keep at it; this can take some time. Beware: It is difficult to determine when all the coating has been removed. When it looks as though the boot leather is wet, you are almost there. Once the leather starts to get wet you must be very careful to change to a soft cloth so that you do not scratch the leather.

3) To test if the coating is off, let the leather of the boot dry **NATURALLY. NEVER** put polish on wet leather; the leather will mold. Don't try to hurry the drying process by putting it in the oven at a really low heat. There is a substantial risk of damaging the boots. Once the leather is dry, apply a small amount of polish to the tip of the boot to make sure it soaks in and polishes to a shine.

Now put the boots on and walk a few steps. If the coating is **not** off, the polish you just added will crack — sometimes the polish will just fall off. If you do not initially see any cracks, walk some more to make sure.

4) If you **DO** see some cracks, repeat step two and continue until there are no cracks.

5) These steps are the same if you ever have to strip boots down.

6) Once boots are thoroughly dry, proceed to the next step, polishing them.

Polishing Boots

After each use, boots will **always** be shined according to this Protocol.

Supplies:
- Saddle soap
- Rag
- Clean cloth, 100% cotton — preferably cheesecloth
- Soft Polish brush
- Small bowl of water
- Black boot polish

Actions to take:

1) Make sure the boots are clean: I do not want you to polish in any dirt. The slave will use saddle soap to clean the boots. Saddle soap will foam. This foam helps to remove the dirt from the leather (making it easy to get off). Now, using a damp rag, remove all the saddle soap and let the boots dry

thoroughly.

2) Before proceeding, the slave will wash hands with soap and water, as body oil — and oils in general — will inhibit formation of the shine.

3) Next, she will put a small amount of polish on her fingers (applying polish with fingers puts the slave more in touch with the process). Using small circular motions, apply polish to the boots until they are covered. Use a brush to bring out the polish in the boots.

4) For a high shine, add polish to clean cheesecloth, then lightly dip it in water and polish the area. As the end approaches, the slave will notice that the cloth will glide increasingly easily over the polished area. As a variant, add saliva to the polish on the cloth. Some Masters may wish that the polish is applied by the slave's tongue. [Note #1: For this shine the slave must NOT use a brush, as this will leave streaks in the polish. Note #2: If the slave applies the polish with her tongue, Lincoln Polish is rumored to have a better taste than Kiwi®. Officer Wes points out that this is odd, because Kiwi® is a Sara Lee brand and Lincoln Polish® is a Sara Lee product.]

Extra Care for Boots

The slave is directed to attend to certain details of this ritual, as Leatherfolk will notice the little things that are *not done,* such as the boot's eyelet, sole and even the boot's tongue.

1) Use a permanent marker to blacken the eyelets. The slave will be very careful not to let the marker touch the leather.

2) Use a toothbrush to get into the hard-to-get to places, such as where the sole meets the leather of the boot. This spot is really hard to reach, so use a little polish on the brush.

3) The slave will use a black candle to cover severe scratches in the boot. Caution: the candle must be black all the way through (not just a top layer of black coloring on a white or clear candle). Let some candle wax pool, then drip the wax onto the scratch — smooth the boot surface.

4) The slave will use edge dressing on the side of the boot's sole. Again, be careful not to get any of dressing on the leather. Edge dressing is **paint** and it is bad for leather.

Note: Kiwi® makes a Heel and Sole Edge Color Renew. It is sold in an applicator bottle. Be careful not to get it on any other surface. The slave will work on a surface well protected with newspaper — which is where the boots belong while they are drying.

When the edge dressing is finished, the slave will rinse off the applicator brush and dry it before putting it away. The applicator will last longer this way.

General Tips:

- Never use any kind of "instant shine" spray. It is just *spray paint* and it cannot be removed from the leather. It will dye the leather — and then you've got a major problem.

- Do NOT use any type of "easy care" products; they are not good for the leather.

- If you take boots to the shoe store to be re-dyed, be sure to tell them NOT to put a top coat on your leather.

- Do NOT ever put a water resistant spray on your leather. Instead, use a product such as Dubbin®. This will protect your leather and will make it water resistant.

- If boots start to develop a foul odor, sprinkle some baking soda in them and leave it there overnight.

Care of Leather Clothing

This protocol instructs the slave in ways of taking care of softer leather items such as vests, pants, jackets and gloves. The slave will inspect all my leather clothing after each use. She will use her judgment to determine whether or not any piece needs care.

1) Never work on wet leather. To avoid causing creases or cracking, always lay these items flat or on a hanger to dry. Always be careful to keep my leather out of the sun.

2) Examine the leather. If the slave finds any portion that is fading, use a soft shoe polish to bring back the color. The softer the polish, the better it will soak into the leather. It will take an hour or two for the leather to soak up all the polish into its pores.

3) Leather cream or Dubbin® can be applied directly on top of polish. Dubbin® will really bring out the leather's luster. If the leather quickly soaks up the Dubbin®, the slave will add another coat the next day, after the leather has had ample time to soak up the first application.

Tips:
If the slave finds that some of my leather has developed mildew, report to me immediately and we will discuss how she let this happen and how she intends to make amends.

By way of remedy, the slave will take one cup of water and one cup of rubbing alcohol on a sponge and work the affected area. Let it dry completely, then use saddle soap to clean the area. Polish and add Dubbin®.

For salt stains, use 1 cup hot water and 1 tablespoon of white vinegar and rub on affected area let dry, clean, polish and condition.

Equipment Care
Clean my floggers by sponging (not soaking) with a solution of warm water to which 5% dishwashing liquid has been added. Be sure to dry the leather thoroughly by squeezing and blotting the falls with paper towels. Do not use any artificial form of heat. Leather does not like to get wet and will remain stiff if not dried adequately.

If the floggers need to be decontaminated, use an ample supply of 70% Isopropyl alcohol, scrubbing with a soft brush if body fluids need to be removed. Spin the whip to aid in the natural process of evaporation/drying.

After cleaning and decontaminating the flogger, restore the natural oils to the falls by using "leather dressings" such as Dubbin®, Lexol® or Pecards®. For floggers other than black, be sure to use a neutral color product. Also be sure the flogger is dry before applying a small amount of the dressing. The slave will work this dressing into the falls with bare hands, allowing a couple of hours for absorption; wipe off any excess with a soft cloth. Allow the flogger to hang after this treatment.

For insertables, after every use, wash in 90% Isopropyl alcohol. Put all cleaned toys away where they belong. Wash all sheets and towels used in play using bleach, if necessary.

Personal Care of Master
Bathing Preparations
Ensure that bath or shower is prepared with:
- Razor designated for shaving my head
- Antibacterial shaving cream
- Bar of aromatic soap — preferably musk or sandalwood scents
- Head and Shoulders® shampoo

Inside the bathroom, in general, preparations include ensuring:
- Bathroom candles are lit (after trimming, if necessary)
- Scene music is playing
- Overhead lights have been dimmed, as appropriate
- Bath mat is placed outside the shower or beside the bath
- Bath towels are within easy reach

Bath
Light candles in bathtub areas, remembering to trim the wicks, if necessary. Draw bath water to temperature of 104 degrees (using meat thermometer to verify). Ask Master which bath salts, etc, he wishes added; add same. Place bath mat beside bathtub and place towels within easy reach of bathtub. Have wine or cocktail prepared and positioned by bathtub. After bath, clean the bathtub with cleanser and remove all accoutrements (glasses, etc.) from the area.

Dressing
Master will direct the slave to organize specific clothing required for the day or evening. Slave will set this clothing out, along with underwear/ socks and shoes, as is customary. Slave will assist Master in dressing, including zipping/buttoning pants and shirt.

Preparing the Bedroom at Night
There are two bedtime protocols for the slave. The first is to turn down the comforter and sheets on my side of the bed; second is to "smudge" the room with sage bundles prepared for that purpose.

The protocol for smudging the room is to close the bedroom door, to light the smudge bundle and to walk around the room smudging the outside perimeter. (Note: Please take care not to over-smudge the room. If it becomes "over-smudged" please air it out some. The room should have a faint lingering scent of sage.

Driving and Car Maintenance
In certain instances, the slave will serve as my chauffeur. This will include proper dress as a chauffeur, including cap and blazer. The slave will also be responsible for the vehicle. The slave will ensure proper vehicle maintenance, including monitoring the need for oil changes and having them done every 3,000 miles. The slave will keep the car's interior spotless and the car floors vacuumed. She will also keep the car washed on a regular basis.

Shopping
The slave will keep the shopping list updated. When any item is used up, it must be listed. Heavily used items should have back-up quantities stored (applesauce, plastic wrap…).

Meats: The slave will take care to purchase high-quality meats, attending to the grade of the meat (prime beef preferred) and the amount of marbling.

Fruits and vegetables: Master prefers that certain items *always* be available in the house — including: apples, mushrooms, black seedless grapes, celery, bananas, parsley and salad fixings. Items such as asparagus, parsley and celery must be stored in water in the refrigerator.

Chef Services
This slave is expected to become a gourmet cook. It is expected that the slave will become particularly adept at the art of *presenting* food on a plate and on a table. This slave is expected to identify relevant

courses of study, locally, nationally, or internationally and present them to Master for consideration.

Kitchen Management

At Master's expense, the slave is expected to purchase and maintain cooking pots, pans, utensils and equipment needed to fulfill this Task. This includes subscribing to specialty publications and catalogs and purchasing requisite cookbooks.

The slave is expected to know and to follow correct procedures for storing wines. This includes organizing our wines and turning them while in storage.

Food Pairing Preferences

Over the years, I have developed tastes for certain condiments with certain foods. That list is as follows:

Food	Condiment
Pork	Applesauce
Lamb	Mint Jelly
Roast Beef	Spiced Peach; Spiced Mango
Pot Roast	Applesauce, Potato pancakes
Turkey, Chicken	Cranberry sauce

As my slave learns more about preparing foods professionally, this section will be expanded.

Storing and Packaging Foods

It is my protocol to wrap foods in Saran® wrap (use only Saran® wrap, not a competitor — Master is concerned about plasticizers in certain brands of cling wrap) or to place them in the appropriate sized plastic storage container before placing them in the refrigerator. That is, if food has been brought back from a restaurant or if food is left over from a meal, it is to be stored in such a way as to maximize the storage life and minimize air contact. At no time is a "take-home" box to be placed in the refrigerator; the food that has been brought home is to be individually wrapped and stored.

Executive Secretary Services

The slave is Master's representative in many domains, including those times when she answers the phone for Master.

Telephone Protocols

Answering the telephone

The slave is Master's representative. Treat this role seriously. Endeavor to answer the phone by the third ring. Always answer the phone by standing (or when standing). Before speaking, SMILE. Use a friendly voice; speak slowly and enunciate clearly.

Say: "Good morning" (or "good afternoon" or "good evening") "This is Dr. Rubel's home, how may I assist you?"

Conversation options

The slave recognizes the caller and knows that Master wishes to take the call: "Yes Ma'am (or "Yes, Sir") I'll get Master."

The slave recognizes the caller but is not sure that Master wishes to take the call: "Sir (or "Ma'am") I'll need to see whether Master can take this call right now."

The slave doesn't recognize the caller: "Ma'am (or "Sir") this is Dr. Rubel's assistant, how may I assist you?

The slave recognizes the caller and KNOWS that Master doesn't wish to have this conversation at this time: "Sir," (or "Ma'am") Master is deeply involved in a project right now and has left Instructions not to be disturbed. May I take a message?"

Taking messages

A formal message pad will be found by the bed in the Master bedroom and on Master's desk, under the telephone. Pens will be with each message pad. In the kitchen, the message pad is in the same drawer as the scissors.

If the slave can't get to the formal message pad, the slave MUST transfer the message to a pad so that the note left will stand out from other scraps of paper.

The message should include: the person's full name (unless you know that I know this person — if there is the *slightest doubt* take down the name). VERIFY LAST NAME SPELLING. The telephone number (verify that the call is local or obtain the area code.) Read the number back to the caller to verify its accuracy. Record the subject of the call (don't be shy in asking; you are my representative).

The message MUST be placed on Master's desk — preferably on the computer keyboard (subtlety won't work in this case).

Preparing Letters

General comment: Master generally prepares his own letters. If the slave is asked to prepare a letter, it will NOT be sent until Master has read it for tone and content.

Font, font size, margins
- Margins: 1.2" all the way around
- Font style: Arial
- Font size: 11 point on 13 pica leading

Style comments: The tone of the letter will be formal but conversational. The letter should sound as though you're *speaking* with the other person. Be concise; don't be chatty.

Preparing Briefing Memos for Master

Master requires a specific format for *one page* "briefing memos." My slave will follow this format:
- Background (what led up to this memo)
- Facts (be careful to keep *opinion* out of this section)
- Alternatives (the first alternative is always: "Do nothing")
- Recommendation (with justification)

Maintain Insurance

Our basic house insurance includes: fire, casualty, umbrella coverage and contents insurance. There is a rider on this policy covering my photographic equipment. The slave will familiarize herself with this policy and discuss any questions she my have. Ensure that new purchases are added to insurance addendum — particularly photographic equipment.

Car insurance: Review annually to ensure relevant coverage.

Major medical insurance is carried through XYZ Insurance Company.

An Evening Out

The slave will ask Master for direction on the general type of evening to be planned. If it is a dinner, the slave will inquire as to the type of food, level of service and price range that Master intends. The slave will also ask about the kind of entertainment sought, if any. This could include theater, cinema, music, dance, or other.

The slave will conduct relevant research and inform Master of the key options (best 2–3 choices) and, upon Instruction, the slave will make relevant reservations.

Planning for Trips

Please refer to Appendix C for an example of our "pre-trip checklist."

Making reservations: Master recommends using Priceline (www. Priceline.com) or similar hotel search engine for reservations. Master prefers a four-star hotel.

On-site Logistics: After reservation have been made, call that hotel's *Concierge* and ask: What are the "don't miss" places in the city and "What special and romantic" restaurants can he/she recommend. Master likes really interesting places. High visual. Interesting foods. Conduct necessary Internet searches for that city/location. In particular, do Google and Yahoo searches for photo sites that may highlight that area.

Air Flights: For Southwest Air, via internet: http://www.southwest.com; for other air reservations use my CitiTravel membership. See me for access codes.

Prepare "Munchies" for trip. This includes: raisins, dates, nuts, candy bars, power bars etc.

Prepare a folder containing all key information, such as maps and *detailed* directions to the hotel and/or activities we will be attending. If we're driving, any places to stop along the way that are *interesting.* All relevant hotel, car rental and airline contact and confirmation numbers must be in this folder. CRITICAL: The "weather report sheet" must be in the folder, too.

Ensure that I have obtained adequate cash/travelers checks: Verify balances on all credit cards that we're taking along.

Courtesan Services

The tradition of the "Courtesan" comes from ancient Greece and Rome. It reappeared in 14th century Renaissance Italy, was later brought to the French Court and continued as a tradition in post-Revolutionary France until the late 1800s. Courtesans, women serving the Royal Court, were schooled in the finest and best of the Female Arts. Courtesans glided; they did not walk. They always knew *le mot juste* for any situation. They spoke elegantly, dressed elegantly, walked elegantly, were excellent hostesses, accomplished lovers, brilliant conversationalists, exhibited great wit and charm, and were extraordinarily seductive. Many were excellent writers, musicians, artists and dancers. These skills are similar to what one might expect of a Geisha — the way she dresses, wears her hair and makeup, the way she walks, moves, talks, entertains, and converses. It's the Total Package.

In this country, short of having grown up among the social aristocracy, having been groomed for a socially prominent marriage, and having attended some type of charm school or finishing school, these kinds of personal behaviors in a woman are extremely rare. Thus, an adult female slave may need quite a bit of exposure to new educational experiences and a huge dose of self-focus and concentration to master Courtesan or Geisha skills. It also takes an Owner who is interested in investing the considerable time, money and effort to form his slave into this sort of art piece.

Personal Appearance and Behavior
Speaking/Gesturing
The slave will be sensitive to the differences in the connotations of words. Word connotation affects both the tone and temper of a person's projected being. For example, in English, one "speaks with" or one "talks to." As one "talks to" a subordinate, this form of oral communication

is closed to my slave when she's communicating with me. She may or may not elect to talk to her daughter, as that is not my concern. This point concerns *tone* and *attitude*. It also concerns *unconscious communication* with Others. That is, there is risk in mindless talking as opposed to purposeful speaking. As *mindfulness in all things* is a key concept for the Courtesan, these points are relevant.

When speaking, the slave will modulate her voice to be as pleasant as possible — never loud, bossy or overbearing. She will avoid using a high nasal voice, and will avoid chattering, mumbling, or whining. She will speak slowly and with a strong voice in order to command attention and respect — while being appropriately deferential.

The slave will avoid using excessive arm or hand movements, as these can be distracting to others and detract from the discussion. The slave will also be as lucid and eloquent as possible, using the fewest and most effective words to convey her thoughts. This is where a large vocabulary (previously discussed) comes into play. She will always be aware of the effect of her words on others (direct meaning as well as connotation) and be keenly aware of when to change the subject or when to stop speaking altogether.

Many times there will be non-verbal clues from listeners reflecting their conversational comfort level. While my slave should be sensitive to these cues, she should not feel as though she needs to carry the conversation alone. The most effective method is to get Others to speak about themselves. I've already mentioned that one of my core values states: "It's more important to be interested than interesting." But even with that basic understanding, members of this Family are to keep abreast of current events as much as possible in order to have *Something to Say* in social settings.

Walking:
The slave will walk in a graceful manner at all times without making undue noise or causing attention to be drawn to her. She will take light steps and she will not bounce; she will glide as though balancing a book on her head. Legs should be kept close together with one foot placed in front of the other. Arms should move from the elbows, not from the shoulder.

Entering and Exiting Vehicles

The proper way to enter a vehicle is first to sit on the car seat facing outwards with legs together, then rotate the body into the car *as a unit* to end up facing forward. When exiting, reverse the process. The slave will rise to a standing position using her legs, not her upper body.

Entering and exiting *trucks* poses more of a challenge since the use of a running board is usually required to enter the cab of the pickup. The slave will always wait for Master to open the car door for the slave, unless instructed otherwise.

Sitting

Sitting at Table: When sitting at Table the slave will be seated in an upright position, legs together. The slave will not slouch or place elbows on the table during the meal. Hands are usually kept in the lap when not eating. When being seated the slave will always enter from the left, arise from the right. Physically, the slave will lower herself to the edge of the chair and then center her torso on the seat surface, adjusting the chair position forward or back as necessary. Legs are kept together with feet crossed at the ankles. (Note: As previously covered, it is our protocol that the slave is always seated by Master at Table. However, after being seated initially (and after the "coming present" ceremony, the slave will have to rise to serve the meal and, throughout the meal, may have to rise to refill water or wine glasses.)

Sitting other than at Table: Here, the slave is responsible for exhibiting grace and elegance in motion. She expected to exude "ladylike demeanor."

Makeup/Hair/Nails

Makeup should never be garish or applied in a heavy manner, unless it's for a certain reason, such as an appearance at a fetish party or for a photographic session where heavier makeup may be called for. Colors used should be appropriate for the color and skin type of the slave. Hair should be washed frequently and kept neatly coiffed in a style that pleases Master. Coloring may be used at Master's discretion. Nails should be manicured on a regular basis. Use of professionally-applied acrylics is permitted, but not required. Use of colored polish on the nails is also permitted.

Dress/Clothing/Perfume

Evening Dress has already been covered; day dress shall generally be all black (Master also tends to wear black during the day). Perfume should be used in moderation; do not overwhelm Master with scent. Master loves Women, not necessarily *perfume.*

Hostess Skills

The slave is expected to serve as Master's Hostess. She is expected to make the guests feel as welcomed as possible and attempt to anticipate their needs in advance. Some guests may have special needs, such as dietary restrictions or health issues that may have to be addressed by tailoring food selections to their requirements. For those who visit often, it is always a sign of extreme respect to have their favorite items on hand for their use. The slave shall keep a 3-ring binder listing special guest needs, and alphabetized by the guest's name, better to ensure advanced preparation for subsequent visits. This listing will include items such as physical or dietary needs. These are also butler skills.

Entertainment

The slave is expected to entertain Master. She is expected to have existing musical and/or voice skills and to develop and improve them in order to bring pleasure both to Master and to herself. To reinforce the importance of this skill, Master will make time available for his slave to take further music and/or voice lessons and to maintain her skill through appropriate practice.

In addition to musical skills, the slave is expected to be able to dance and to learn different styles of dance in order to please Master and to serve him as a dance partner. Master will arrange that dance lessons be taken to gain new skills in this area.

Artistic and Literary Pursuits

The slave is expected to have skills in the arts. She is expected to be skilled in areas such as oral recitation, writing, painting, photography, flower arranging, calligraphy, needlework or other areas of Master's interest. This furthers the slave's personal growth and brings delight to Master when his slave is personally fulfilled to her greatest potential. Classes in any of these areas are greatly encouraged. Additionally, the slave is expected to assist Master in researching and writing whenever requested.

Indoor/Outdoor Recreational Activities

The slave is expected to participate in outdoor activities: She will maintain her body in such a way as to be able to participate in outdoor activities. She is also expected to have or to obtain some degree of knowledge and skill regarding various outdoor recreational activities and team sports.

Though this might not typically be considered to fall within the category of Courtesan or Geisha skills, in this day and age, it's important that the slave to be well-rounded and flexible so that she can enjoy a wide range of social situations. The occasion may arise when I wish my slave to participate in some activity. This may include baseball, basketball, biking, camping, fishing, hiking, horseback riding, ice skating, playing pool, playing cards and board games, roller skating, snow skiing, water sports, swimming, tennis or volleyball, croquet, shuffleboard and the like. Not only will the slave be physically prepared for these activities, but will know enough about them to be able to participate.

Sexual Techniques

The slave is expected to be thoroughly knowledgeable (and widely read) in the art of lovemaking.

Related to that, the slave is expected to continue her daily practice of strengthening her pelvic floor muscles by performing Kegel exercises and to continue to master the art of "deep throating."

Healing Arts

The slave is expected to use her gifts in the healing arts. This includes keeping her nursing license current and continuing to learn and to master specialty areas such as Reiki, hypnosis and other alternative healing techniques and practices. She is expected to use these gifts for the benefit of Master and Others.

An M/s Studies Book

Epilogue

Some Thoughts for Readers

Live in the Present

Recently, a woman was being interviewed on National Public Radio. Her husband had just died. With an obvious tremor in her voice, she commented that: "The five months since he died have been longer than the 58 years we were married."

This grabbed me. I realized just how important my relationship with my slave has become, how important she is to me. Every evening is *special* because we both work hard to make it so. I hope that this book has given you some ideas to adapt to your own lives and loves.

Many Try It, Few Succeed

Unfortunately, M/s relationships are known for their brevity. They seldom last. If you look at those few that DO last, the couples are generally very mature (in age) and have been married a time or two. They know what worked and what didn't work in "Vanilla" relationships and they've been through enough personal self-examination (with or without a therapist) to know how to work with (manage?) their partner over the long term.

In important ways, the fantasy of a Master/slave relationship differs from the reality of it. Conducting a Master/slave play scene differs from the reality of living 24/7 in the M/s culture. From the Master's viewpoint, it takes work to feed the emotional needs of the person serving as the slave. And the Master must appreciate that every act of obedience, every act of service, is a gift to him from his slave. What does Master offer that earns this kind of Gift, this kind of Honor, Respect and Devotion? The Master has to appreciate why it would be that someone would make this bargain with him.

Take a step back and look at what you've been reading in this book. Consider, for a moment, that every bit of it is real. My slave is serving as my valet, butler, chef, secretary, hostess, entertainer, research assistant, nurse, healer, maid, kinky play partner and sex partner extraordinaire. This is a full-time job. The added responsibility of working outside the home and caring for her biological family in a Vanilla setting means she is working overtime. It takes a tremendous commitment on everyone's part to keep these worlds separate.

So, both Master and slave have to be really, really clear about the goal, the Purpose of this kind of *structured relationship.* Both adults must be psychologically stable and be working in unison to support life within the M/s dynamic.

Considering the slave for a moment, there's a vast difference from *thinking* you would like to be a slave and *having a slaveheart.* Unless this relationship structure grabs your heart AND your mind, it's not likely to work very long. But this is something each of you has to find out on your own. If you haven't already done so, I recommend reading Guy Baldwin's book *Slavecraft.* Read it slowly and read it more than once. Also read Guy Baldwin's *Ties that Bind.* Then, start attending the regional and national Master/slave conferences (there are five regional feeder conferences and one International M/s conference at this writing — Appendix F). Read extensively on the few *real* Leather websites you can find. If you are lucky enough to live near a chapter of MAsT (Masters and slaves Together), join it.

Leathersex: The Goal of it All.

The *spiritual dynamic* is, in my opinion, one of the defining differences between *Leather* and *Not-Leather.* As Guy Baldwin puts it: "When leather and SM scenes were done in a certain way, we achieved a different level of awareness — we felt transformed into someone whom it felt better to be. Also, a kind of bonding occurred between SM players that had been missing in our more usual sexual encounters." (*Ties that Bind* p. 34). What I will add here, is that after sufficient practice at sexual play techniques, it is not uncommon for my sexual partner to go into subspace from these activities alone — absent any SM. I live for the surprise they later express at this. This is called "sex magic" and although it's whispered about, it's hard to find much written about it. You may start with *Sensuous Magic* by Pat Califia and *Secrets of Western Sex Magic* by Frater U∴D∴ Of these two, the latter is more on-point.

And That's a Wrap

I hope you've enjoyed this book. It's a window into another culture. Some readers will appreciate the view; others are likely to condemn me for having written it. At its core, this is an etiquette book with an attitude. Readers should feel free to write to me with questions at PowerExchangeEditor@yahoo.com. In the subject line, please put the phrase: ***book contact***.

An M/s Studies Book

Appendices

An M/s Studies Book

Appendix A

Example of Training Contract

Initial Contract For Consensual slave Training

Dated: _____

Preamble

This Contract is between_____, hereinafter referred to as Master, and _____, hereinafter referred to as *the slave*.

(This next line was included in this actual Contract: *This Contract is offered directly between _____ and _____ and lives outside the Leather Family structure to which _____ _____ is party.*)

Caveat

This contract is in no way legally binding, and is meant only as an aid better to understand the needs, duties and responsibilities of _____ _____ and _____ as they begin a period of slave training.

Commitment and Termination

I, _____, hereinafter referred to as *the slave*, do of my own free will, and being of sound mind and body, hereby offer myself in consensual training to _____, hereinafter referred to as Master, for the period beginning _____ and ending on _____, unless extended or terminated in writing at a different date. Either party may terminate this Contract at any time before the above named date only in the event of a material breach. Prior to _____, this Contract will be reviewed, renegotiated and rewritten, or terminated.

Contract Provisions

1) To the best of this slave's ability, this slave pledges to honor the terms and the spirit of this Contract and to study and develop the skills and knowledge necessary to serve Master's wishes and desires. This service will be without ego, pride or expectations. From this day until the termination or extension of this Contract, this slave Pledges at all times to obey Master with humility and to subvert her will and desires to his Will and Desires. To the extent possible, this slave will hide nothing from him and answer all Questions fully and honestly.

2) During this period of Training, the slave agrees to obey Master to the best of her ability, and to devote herself entirely to Master's pleasure, whether through readings, writings, dress, personal service or sexual service. This slave also renounces all rights to her own pleasure, comfort, or gratification except insofar as permitted by him. The slave agrees to learn what interests and excites Master through exploration and communication, and to incorporate such discoveries into this relationship.

3) Master now accepts full responsibility for this slave. This includes — but is not limited to — this slave's emotional, physical and mental well-being. This slave accepts full responsibility for informing Master of all fears, concerns and anxieties on any and all topics, and also to inform him of any real or perceived dangers or safety concerns, whether or not they relate directly to him or to them as a couple. Concurrently, this slave recognizes and agrees that Master's decisions on any topic represent the final word regarding the resolutions of such issues. The slave will not be punished for respectfully stating these concerns. Master strives to listen to slave concerns with a clear and open heart and mind.

4) The slave agrees to dress in the styles and fashions selected by Master, and Master does not make such dress requirements of this slave as to represent financial hardship or burden.

5) During this trial period, we will play by SSC rather than RACK rules. That is, the slave agrees to accept responsibility for using safewords or safe gestures when necessary. The slave acknowledges that the *physical play* safeword is **red** and that

the *emotional* safeword is Master's given name. Master accepts the responsibility for stopping activities in progress to assess situations where the slave uses a safeword, and he will, to the best of his ability, immediately modify or stop the activity. The slave agrees to hold no ill will due to his decision. Master will not punish the slave for the use of a safeword or safe gesture.

6) The slave agrees to answer fully and promptly any and all questions asked by Master. This is a **FULL DISCLOSURE** Contract. Further, this slave agrees to **volunteer** any information that Master *should know* regarding the slave's physical, mental or emotional state. Master will not use this information to harm the slave in any way.

7) The slave has previously stated her limits in a checklist and Master will not violate these limits without prior negotiation with and consent by the slave.

8) The slave agrees to address _____ as Master unless otherwise directed. The slave agrees to abide by such Manual of Protocol as is ultimately created for her. The slave agrees to speak respectfully to him at all times, including times not spent in a scene. Master may address the slave in any way he chooses.

9) Master will furnish the slave with such token(s) of ownership as he sees fit; the slave agrees to wear such symbol(s) at all times, except when he states to do so would be inappropriate or would non-consensually involve others.

10) The slave agrees not to have any sexual encounter other than with Master for the duration of this Contract, unless permission has been granted in advance, and that she will not engage in self-pleasuring actions without requesting specific prior permission from Master.

11) The slave agrees and understands that minor infractions of this Agreement will be dealt with through *Correction* and that continued inappropriate behavior or material breach of contract will be Punished by withdrawing attention for a specified period and/or by administering manageable physical discipline in private. Any Correction or Punishment will end in debriefing and forgiveness.

12) If the slave commits an act that violates the trust that Master has placed in her, a third party (selected by Master if not mutually agreed upon) will be chosen to hear the issue and to administer a Consequence.

- The slave agrees to abide by any Ruling made in such a case.
- There will be a debriefing and forgiveness that will complete the cycle.
- Time with this slave-in-training must not take away from established times with members of Master's Leather Family.

Fluid Bonding

Fluid bonding may occur once these terms and conditions have been met.

- Slave must test negative for all STDs in a test taken at an appropriate time after last sexual encounter.
- Slave must agree that ALL future sex partners are **pre-negotiated** with Master.
- Slave must agree that ALL future sex partners will use condoms during intercourse.
- If the slave lapses in striving for obedience, she will return to a state of obedience by immediately bringing this — like any other lapse — to Master's attention.
  - In the event of an episode of unprotected sex, there will then be a period of protected sex between this slave and Master sufficient to enable this slave to be retested for STDs and to obtain test results.

Master will...

1) Use the slave in any way he so desires, and for any purpose he desires;

2) Encourage the slave to explore her slaveheart;

3) Serve as a Guide for the slave in her quest for submission and spiritual connection through BDSM;

4) Give the slave Directives and Instructions that may carry beyond their physical time together;

5) Provide the slave such tokens of ownership as he chooses; and

6) Correct inappropriate behavior in whatever manner he chooses. Such correction will end in debriefing and forgiveness.

Accepted, understood and agreed to this _____ day of_____, 20__.

_____, Master

_____, slave

Appendix B

The Safe Call

A safe call is a prearranged agreement with an outside party whose job is to call the police and to get help if they don't hear from the person by a particular time. It should be used any time you are planning a first meeting with someone. Often, it is used for second or third meetings as well — or until you feel you know this person reasonably well. *Whenever you use a safe call, be sure that the person you intend to meet knows that you are using this procedure.* It would be impolite for you to meet someone for the first time and — without letting the person know you're using these procedures — have to say: "Excuse me, I have to make my safe call right now."

Typically, subs set up the safe call, although a Dom/Domme may arrange them as well. You gather all of the pertinent information such as name, address, phone number, driver's license number, etc., from your prospective partner and deliver it to a third party. You then set a time by which the third party must be contacted. If the call isn't made then the third party calls the police, tells them that you might have been taken captive, and then gives them the pertinent information.

There are a few more details to a safe call. One is that the caller typically has a non-obvious phrase or password to indicate that they are safe. This way, even if they end up being held hostage and are forced to make the safe call, they can still alert the third party. Secondly, the caller lets their prospective partner know that a safe call has been arranged. The only thing that the prospective partner should know is at what time the call needs to be made. (Be careful, time flies when playing. Set an alarm on your cell phone to remind you.) It should raise a red flag if the prospective partner presses for more information and/or tries to dissuade you from setting up the safe call. An ethical person won't mind having a safe call in place — but remember: you must have notified your play partner that you're using safe call procedures. Third, YOU should plan to arrive at least 15 minutes early so that you can park and get to the meeting place before your prospective date. You don't want this person to be able to identify your car or vehicle license number. Similarly, you should watch this person leave before you approach your car.

Basic information is:

- Name and physical description of the person

- Driver's license number (you should have your prospective partner fax you a copy of the DL — how do you know it is a valid DL number?)

- Phone number where you will be meeting or playing

- Address where you will be meeting and/or playing. (Playing is not recommended for the first meeting.)

- Type of location — home, restaurant, etc.

- When the safe call should be made (When meeting and leaving? Every hour on the hour with only five minutes of grace period? Etc.)

- A non-obvious phrase to indicate that you are safe. (e.g.: "OK, then put on your pajamas and watch a video, I don't care." Means you're safe.)

- Any pertinent details on the meeting that you have arranged

Additional safety notes:

- Meet the first time at a restaurant such as IHOP™, that will have multiple cameras scanning the room. If you feel threatened, you can mention these cameras to the person you're meeting.

- The first time, or maybe even the first few times you play, avoid doing anything that may leave you unable to escape. This would include bondage activities, getting into anyone else's car, and so forth. You can save that type of fun for a later date.

- In this day of Caller ID, submissives in particular may have worries about talking on the phone with a Dom before they're ready to exchange names, addresses, and phone numbers (particularly when they have a listed phone number). If someone gives you a phone number and requests that you call, has Caller ID, and you don't block your phone number from being transmitted, he or she may be able to obtain more information about you than you would like.

- However, your local phone company may allow you to block the transmission of your phone number to the next phone number (ONLY the next phone number) that you dial. Dialing *67 (or 1167 on a rotary phone) accomplishes that where I live. Try it out first with someone you trust, or check for the details about how your phone company does this in your local phone book. It may not be available everywhere.

*This appendix has been created from various Internet sources combined with my own personal experiences. See for example, http://www.bdsm-peergroup.com/about_safe_call_service.htm

An M/s Studies Book

Appendix C

Resources for Dress or for Formal Service

Books on Topics Related to Formal Service
The Art of the Table: a complete guide to table settings, table manners, and tableware. Suzanne von Drachenfels (Simon and Schuster: New York, New York) 2000.

Butlers and Household Managers. Stephen M. Ferry (Booksurge Publishing: North Charleston, South Carolina) 2005.

Service Etiquette, 4th Edition. Orthea D. Swartz (Naval Institute Press: Annapolis, Maryland) 1988.

Shining Combat Boots

http://www.stompersboots.com/stompers_bootcare.php

Equipment Cleaning Tips

http://www.purplepassion.com/purple-passion-hints.html

http://www.heartwoodwhips.com/info.htm

Mens Dress – "Outfits"
For "Mess Dress," I routinely monitor eBay™ under that search heading. This is an extremely reasonable way to come up with truly unusual dinner jackets.

Napkin Folding
There are some beautiful ways to fold napkins. These are among my favorite picks for websites that show you how to do it.

http://kitchen.robbiehaf.com/NapkinFolds.html

http://www.customlinenservice.com/napkins.htm

http://www.butlersguild.com/index.php?subject=44&nm=Napkin%20Folding

Silver, Care and Cleaning

More than you ever wanted to know about maintaining your silver service, brought to you by the Society of American Silversmiths:

http://www.silversmithing.com/care.htm

Table Setting Choices

This robust site provides excellent photos and guidance about flatware and china placement as a function of the number and kind of courses being offered:

http://www.schonwalder.net/Tablesettings/list_a.htm

Uniforms

This is my favorite site for formal serving uniforms. My slave's serving uniforms come from here.

http://www.tipsuniforms.com/tips/catalog/index. php?cPath=2000_2700

For some FABULOUS maid outfits, try:

http://www.frenchmaids4you.com/Maids.htm and

http://www.versatilefashions.com

Wine: Glasses and Serving Temperatures and Tasting:

This site describes every shape of wine glass known to man. Very impressive site:

http://www.diwinetaste.com/english/Serving.php

If you want to learn the correct techniques for tasting wines, try this site:

http://www.thewinedoctor.com/advisory/tastetastingwine.shtml

Wine and Food Pairing

http://www.butlersguild.com/index.php?subject=102&nm=Wine %20&%20Food%20Pairing

Appendix D
Travel Checklist

Trip Location: _____

People Traveling with Master: _____

Trip Dates: _____ Travel by: □ car   □ plane   □ other

Cash obtained for this trip: _____ □ credit card has $_____ available

ITEM	DONE
PREPARE A TRIP FOLDER CONTAINING MEMOS THAT INCLUDE	
Name(s) of hotel(s) for each day, including confirmation #s and local phone #s	
Car rental information, if relevant, including confirmation #s and phone #	
"Weather conditions" report covering all travel days	
Attach a sheet that includes all relevant driving directions and maps	
If entertainment reserved, include all driving directions, times, confirm #s	
PREPARE TRAVEL SNACKS	
Teabags	
Powdered creamer	
Sweet-n-low	
Nuts, raisins, dates, apples, etc	

WALLET	
Business cards	
Family cards	
PACKING ISSUES	
Remove scissors from toiletries bag	
Verify that all pills are in the toiletries bag	
Ensure that we have an adequate supply of business cards	
Verify that there is a notebook and pen in the computer bag	
Pack liquor for hotel room plus shot glass	
Bathing suit	
One pair of socks and underwear per day	
Evening clothes: black dress slacks, dress shoes, black dress shirt and jacket	
Day clothing and shoes/boots – check with Master	
Jackets, raingear – seasonal, depending upon weather; check with Master	
Cell phone charging unit.	
Camera charging units	
Computer battery charged?	
Camera battery charged?	
Extra power supply?	

All reading glasses?	
Beret	
VENDING ISSUES	
Roll of packing tape	
Box cutter	
Rack for books and plastic stand for magazines	
Box of medium binder clips	

An M/s Studies Book

Appendix E

Sexual Stuff

Cunnilingus

http://www.howtohavegoodsex.com/tips_for_the_woman_receiving_cun.htm

Fellatio

http://www.sexinfo101.com/pm_fellatio.shtml

Good basic book: *Tickle his Pickle: your hands-on guide to penis pleasing.* Sadie Allison (Tickle Kitty, Inc: San Francisco, California) 2004 www.ticklekitty.com

More advanced (and very good) book: *The Ultimate Guide to Fellatio.* Violet Blue (Cleis Press: San Francisco, California) 2002 www.goodvibrations.com

Huge Sex-Techniques Resource Sites
These sites are particularly good about teaching stuff to guys about playing with their slaves sexually.

http://www.sex-project.com/1/

http://clitical.com/index.php

Pleasing Your Master
Start with Jay Wiseman's books (Greenery Press: San Francisco, California) *Tricks to Please a Man;More than 125 Ways to Make Good Sex Better*

Sex Positions

http://users.forthnet.gr/ath/nektar/kma/main.htm

http://www.sexualpositionsfree.com/index.html

An M/s Studies Book

Appendix F

Master/slave Conferences

If you intend competing for the International Master/slave title, you first have to win a regional title, then compete again at Southplains Leatherfest in Dallas in February. Here are the related website links:

"Feeder" Conferences

[Note: conferences are listed in order of occurrence after Southplains in February. Thus the Southwest conference appears last because it occurs in January — at the end of the competition cycle for the previous year.]

Northeast (Washington, D.C., July)
http://www.mastertaino.com/Master_slave_Conference.htm

Great Lakes (Indianapolis, August)
http://greatlakesleather.org/web/schedule.html

Northwest (San Jose, CA, TBA)
http://www.folsomfringe.com/start.php

Southeast (Atlanta, GA, June)
http://www.seleatherfest.com/GuestsContest.php

Southwest (Phoenix, January)
http://www.southwestleather.org

Culminating Event
International Master/slave Conference (Dallas, February)
http://www.southplainsleatherfest.com

Important Link
This link will enable you to identify all these websites at one time and also gives the names of current and past titleholders.
It is also an excellent historical site.
http://www.southplainsleatherfest.com/regionals.html

An M/s Studies Book

References

APEX ACADEMY/BUTCHMANNS Protocol for slaves Revised May 1998

Inspired by and incorporating, with permission, material from SlaveMaster Mike McDade's "Principles and Commitment." Copyright © 1998 by Butchmann's Academy; all rights reserved and used in parts of Chapters 1–4 of this book by express permission of Master Steve Sampson. To access this information in its original form, readers are referred to this link:
http://www.arizonapowerexchange.org/academy/protocol/index.html

Officer Wes' Protocols
I have used some material in this book that was originally created by The Good Officer. While it now lives on in a form and format somewhat different from Officer Wes' version, his thinking and writings nonetheless stand as the original material. You can find his protocols at: http://www.westom.com/leather/protocol.htm.

Master Gary McEntyre's Protocols
Master Gary McEntyre was kind enough to give me a copy of his own Protocol Manual. A number of sections from his Manual have been included, here, in their adapted form, principally in Chapters 1 and 2.

Service Etiquette
Some of the material in Chapter 5 was inspired by Service Etiquette, Fourth Edition by Oretha D. Swartz (Annapolis, MD: Naval Institute Press) 1988. There are many similarities between formal military dining protocols and High Leather dining protocols and I found this book to be particularly helpful in pointing out many of the details of such service.

About the Author

Dr. Robert J. Rubel is an educational sociologist and researcher by training. Immediately after college he taught high school English in south-central Los Angeles for three years. Returning to graduate school, he earned an EdM in urban education and a PhD in the area of crime prevention in public schools. After some years working on staff and also serving as a Visiting Fellow for the U.S. Department of Justice, he formed a 501(c)(3) that specialized in research and training in the area of crime prevention in public schools. He ran that firm for 17 years.

In 1985, Dr. Rubel formed the American Association of Wood Turners and built its membership from zero to about two thousand in two years. At that point, the organization was turned over to people who had more time to devote to it. The organization is alive and well to this day.

In his mid-40s, Robert decided to change careers and joined a "boutique" stock brokerage and future brokerage firm in the Georgetown area of Washington, D.C. Within six months, he was made a Principal of the futures brokerage side of the firm and within another six months, named CEO. He ran the company for an additional four years. In the late 1990s, upon the request of a close friend, Dr. Rubel returned to Austin to help start a new company. He worked there as vice president for operations for five years, then retired to pursue his passion as an erotic and fetish art photographer.

Robert Rubel has been involved in the BDSM scene for a number of years, throwing himself into the literature of the field as though it were an academic study. He attends BDSM weekend conferences many times a year. Within his local community, Robert (for the past several years using his professional photography business name of "Corwin") has served on the board of NLA-Austin, a Council Member of SAADE (School for Advanced American-Style Dominants' Education), Director of SAADE's Special Interest Group for Master/slave relations, and for two years, part of the Leadership Core of the Austin Mentors Program — where he also served as a Mentor for fire play and M/s relations.

Currently, Robert is the Managing Editor of Power Exchange Magazine: An Alternative Lifestyle Publication: www.PowerExhangeMagazine.com.

To view Dr. Rubel's erotic and fetish photography, see: www.photosbycorwin.com

To view Dr. Rubel's nature photography, see: www.scenesofbeauty.com

To contact Dr. Rubel about presentations, lectures or questions, use: PowerExchangeEditor@yahoo.com. In the subject line, say: "Book Contact" (this will cause your email to bypass his spam filter).

Other Books by Dr. Rubel
Academic Books:
The Unruly School: disorders, disruptions and crime. Robert J. Rubel (D.C. Heath and Company: Lexington, Massachusetts) 1977.

Violence and Crime in the Schools. Keith Baker and Robert J. Rubel (eds.) (D.C. Heath and Company: Lexington, Massachusetts) 1980.

Kink Books
All books can be obtained from www.PowerExchangeBooks.com.

Flames of Passion: Handbook of erotic fire play. David Walker and Robert J. Rubel, PhD (Booksurge) 2006.

Master/slave Relations: Handbook of Theory and Practice. Robert J. Rubel, PhD (Booksurge) 2006.

Protocol Handbook for the Leather slave: Theory and Practice Robert J. Rubel, PhD (Booksurge) 2006.

Wholes: The Photographic Erotic Art of Robert J. Rubel, PhD. Robert J. Rubel, PhD (Booksurge) 2006.

Holes: The Photographic Erotic Art of Robert J. Rubel, PhD. Robert J. Rubel, PhD (Booksurge) 2006.

Parts: The Photographic Erotic Art of Robert J. Rubel, PhD. Robert J. Rubel, PhD (Booksurge) 2006.

461790

Made in the USA